Anyone CAN Draw!
in Ten Sessions

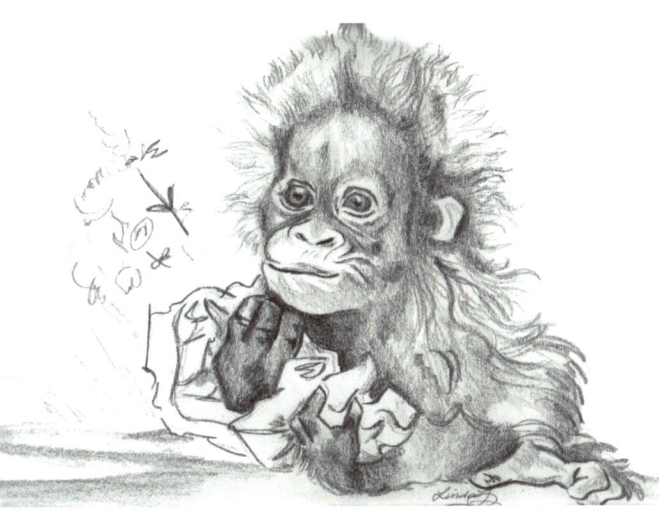

A Hands-on approach to
learning to use your right brain
with skill building exercises
that help anyone draw
what they see

By Linda Laforge

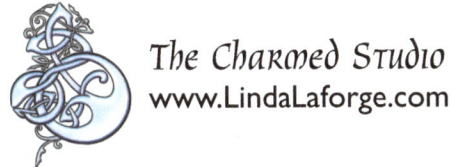

The Charmed Studio
www.LindaLaforge.com

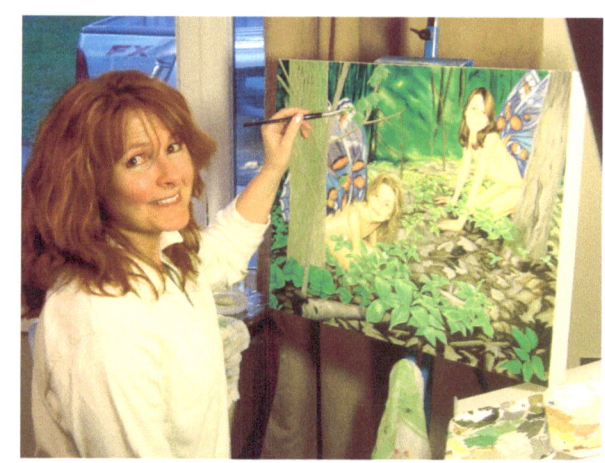

About the Author

Linda Laforge is the author of "Anyone CAN Draw in Ten Sessions". She is primarily a self-taught artist with training in Industrial Design and has been a Graphic Designer for over 18 years. She has taught adults graphic design at Georgian College for several years. She has also taught individuals how to draw since her high school years.

Linda was practically drawing from birth. When she was in grade 3 she wrote short stories, illustrated them and created little books to give to her mother. "In one way or another, I've been doing the same ever since," Laforge says.

Today you can find her drawings and paintings on her website at www.LindaLaforge.com.

ISBN-13: 978-1479169634
ISBN-10: 1479169633

Cover designed by Linda Laforge
Interior design by Linda Laforge

Acknowledgement

Dedicated to anyone who ever wanted to draw, but thought they never could... this book is for you. I hope you enjoy and find inspiration.

Inspired by *Iain McCaig*. An unbelievably creative and skilled professional artist I saw in Philadelphia in October of 2008. He told me that he's always taught drawing to those who never thought they could. A big "aah haa" moment! That's when I realized how important it is to me to share one of my greatest loves.

I found lots of great direction from two books on drawing which completely fit my belief of drawing and art. *"Drawing with your Artist's Brain"* by Carl Purcell and *"How to Draw What You See"* by Rudy De Reyna. Both books helped me to vastly improve my drawing technique and I am eternally grateful. I hope this book does the same for you.

Contents

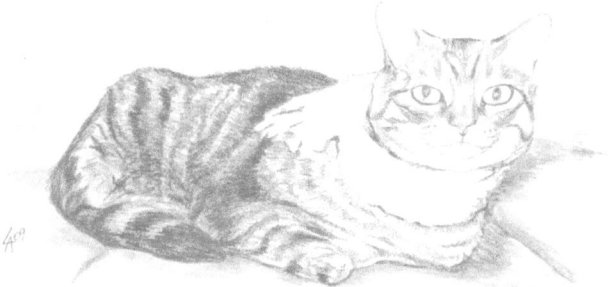

Introduction

Hello wannabe artists! You've taken the first step in learning how to draw... you've got a book. This book! I'm grateful to you for choosing it.

You're going to discover that you're not the only person on the planet who's had the same desire to want to draw. Some very successful and famous (and now dead) artists began completely without talent or ability, as do we all.

Drawing is our first language. We drew from the moment we were able to pick up a crayon or pencil and scribble. We loved it. It was so much fun! It once was lost – and now can be found again.

You're going to discover how your own brain has been messing up your drawing. The best part is, once you realize how it works, everything will begin to change. Your drawing will change as you work through a myriad of exercises designed to help you draw what you see. It will be a fun, creative journey into the world of an artist. Once you've completed all ten sessions, and maybe some more, you should find your drawing has markedly improved. You <u>will</u> be able to draw.

Here's to your new journey!

How this book works!

Every chapter is designed to be a 2 hour drawing workshop, as though you are in a classroom. It should help you to get into the mindset of dedicating the time needed to develop the skills and to learn the drawing techniques available to you right here.

Every session begins with a Warm-up Exercise. That means you get out the drawing paper you're most comfortable working with and start drawing according to instructions. It's purpose is to limber up your hand muscles and help set your mind free, at least a little. The point of the Warm-up is to relax your senses, not to create a perfectly accurate drawing. It's fun! Fun in art is important ... and it's the best way to start your drawing session.

You will find lessons and exercises throughout each Session. Take the time you need to read this information. It explains the point of the exercises you're working on. Each exercise in your Sessions has been given a time limit. Ex. Exercise 1 *(15 minutes)*. It suggests you spend at least 15 minutes on this drawing. If you finish early and feel you've done as requested, great! If you need more time in order to complete the exercise so that you fully 'get' what it's about, that's OK too.

Everyone does have their own drawing pace. Some speed along, like I do (though I've been doing it a long time) and others, even professional artists, work at a nice slow pace. There is no right or wrong, so take whatever time you need. The time suggestions do seem to conform to most classroom norms, which are 2 hours per session.

The beauty of learning from home - you can break when you want to, and get back to it whenever you're ready. Just make sure you keep coming back to it!

Like anything in life, if it's important to you, it's worth the time and effort. Without those two elements, you won't do the exercises needed. As an athlete practices and exercises every day to develop his or her skills in sport to be the best they can be, so must you...

Let's go draw!

Drawing Tools

Sketch Books - ideally 2. One that's 11" x 17" and another around 9" x 12"

You can get all these items in a set or package for less, rather than purchasing each item individually

Set of 8 graphic pencils with varying leads

3 charcoal pencils (optional)

2 charcoal sticks (optional)

1 kneaded eraser

1 pencil sharpener

1 charcoal sharpener (optional)

1 sketch stick

1 blending stick

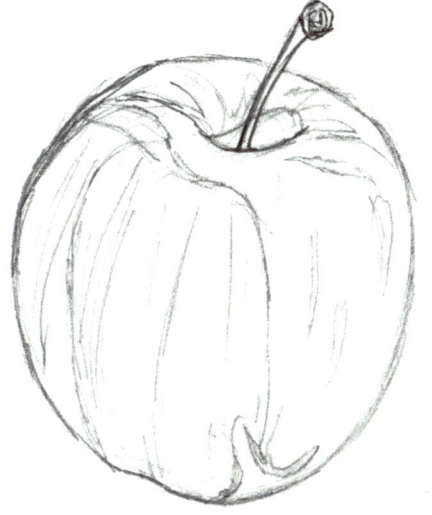

I'd love to see your "Before" and "After" drawings. Once you've completed the workshop, join "Linda Laforge's Anyone Can Draw Facebook Group" and post your drawings! I may even use them in the next edition of this book or on the website.

You'll find the Facebook Group page here:
https://www.facebook.com/135512744590

You'll find some how-to videos on my You Tube page.
Click here to find those!
http://www.**youtube**.com/**LindaLaforgeArt**

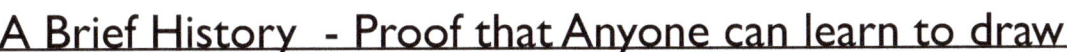

A Brief History - Proof that Anyone can learn to draw

Paul Cézanne ~ January 1839 – October 1906

His father intended that he study law, but Paul Cézanne had other plans. He convinced his Dad to send him to Paris in 1861 where he enrolled in the *Academy Suisse*. Even though he failed the entrance examination to the *School of Fine Arts,* he met Pissarro and Guillaumin. He went back home to work in is father's bank in Aix-en-Provence. He was not a quitter – so returned the following year to Paris and *the School of Fine Arts*.

Cézanne remained a self-educated painter. He was never offered entrance into the *School of Fine Arts*, and the *Swiss Academy* did not give him courses. His first paintings were awkward, inaccurate and some were kinda ugly, in my humble opinion.

Regardless, he worked very hard, and hung with Bazille, Renoir, Monet, Sisley and eventually Manet. He only shared ambition, desire of innovation, and their revolt against the academic standards of the time.

A few befores...

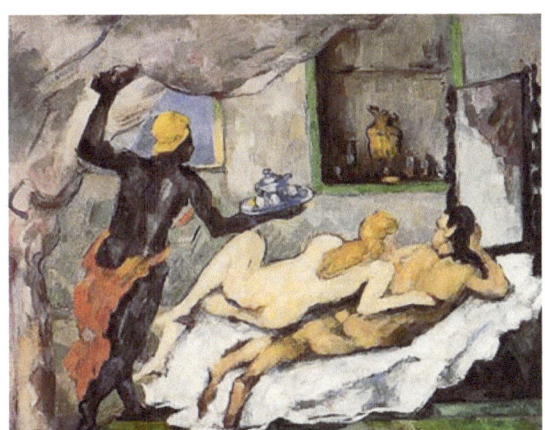

Afternoon in Naples
1875-77,
Oil on Canvas,
National Gallery of Australia,
Canberra,
Australia

Painted when he was 28.

Started painting when he was 36.

The Abduction
1867,
Oil on Canvas,
Fitzwilliam Museum,
Cambridge,
England

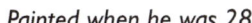

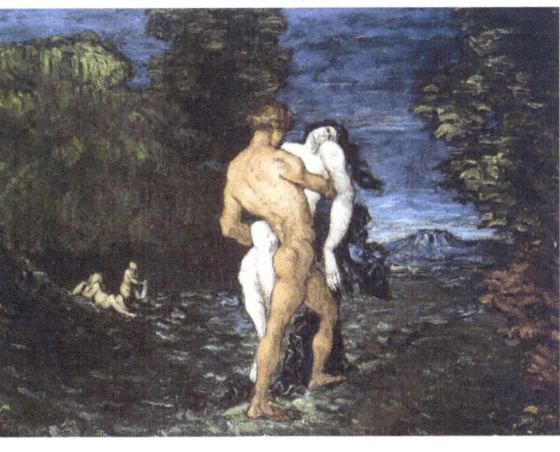

Cézanne decided he could do it – he decided that he was a painter.

He focused a lot of time and effort in doing so – easy for him as Daddy paid his rent and expenses. (Of course, if Daddy knew he had a girlfriend and child he would have cut off the money!) None-the-less, he did it!

One of his paintings was accepted at the Salon in 1882. This constitutes an exception which was not be renewed, and, refused once again in 1884. It was accepted on a technicality - he submitted it as a pupil of Guillemet, thus ducking the jury.

Cézanne eventually "gives up the fight for Paris". He painted nature while out-of-doors. He preferred working reclusively and lived in Aix rather than alternating between the south and Paris. For some reason he preferred living with his Mom and Sister rather than with the mother of his child, and his son. I guess he was focused on his passion - his art!

A few afters...

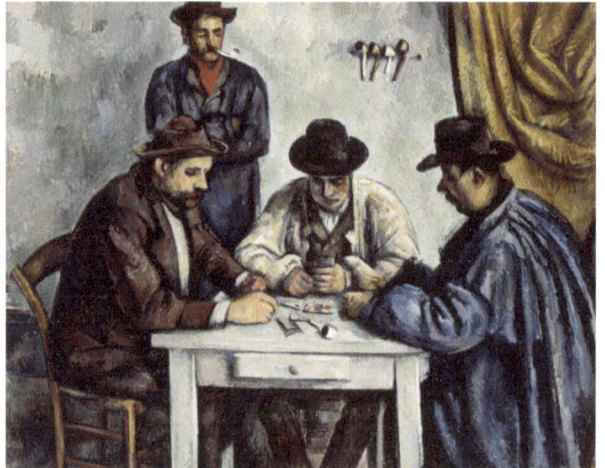

The Card Players
Early 1890's,
Oil on Canvas,
New York: The Metropolitan Museum of Art

Painted when he was 43.

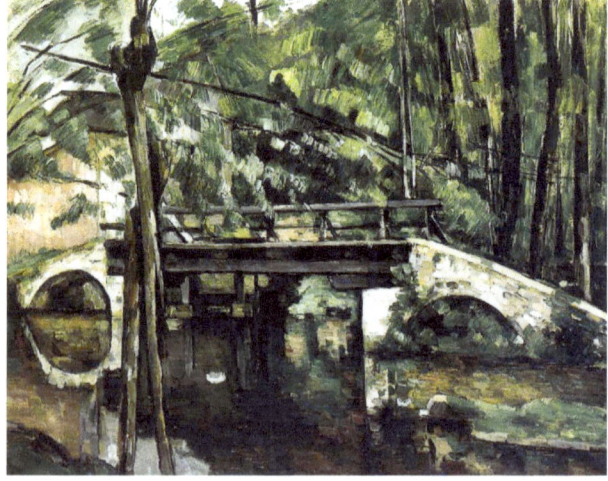

The Bridge of Maincy
c. 1882-85,
Oil on Canvas,
Musée d'Orsay, Paris

Painted when he was 51.

Cézanne was right! He became a fabulous painter. He is now often called the father of modern art.

A Brief History - Proof that Anyone can learn to draw

Vincent Van Gogh ~ March 1853 – July 1890

Son of a Dutch Protestant pastor, Vincent Van Gogh had an uncle who was co-director of an international art dealing company. He began to follow the family tradition by joining Goupil & Co in July 1869. He was to work with Goupil for more than 5 years where he developed a dislike for art trading. He then lived the life of a recluse while reading the Bible intensely. He was a teacher in a small boarding school, then a preacher and evangelist for coal miners of a desolate region. Vincent gave up his vocation as he couldn't seem to mix politics and religion.

In August 1880 at the age of 27, Vincent decided to become a painter.

He was largely self taught. His family paid his way, so he had the same good fortune as Cézanne. Anton Mauze, a cousin, gave him drawing lessons. He began his first paintings in 1882. After his father died he eventually went to Paris to stay with his brother Theo. He had to make a living. There he met Fernand Cormon, Emile Bernard & Henri de Toulouse-lautrec.

During the time of his stay in Arles, from his arrival on February 20, 1888, to his departure for Saint-Remy Mental Hospital on May 8, 1889, Van Gogh created 200 paintings, more than one hundred drawings, and wrote more than 200 letters.

His story is long, interesting and sad. Before he shot himself In July of 1890, he was passionate, prolific and he was truly an artist.

A few befores...
You'll notice his people aren't properly proportioned and his veggies are vague.

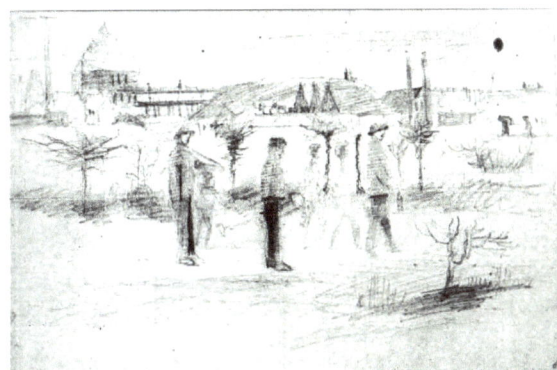

Painted when he was 27.

Miners in the Snow at Dawn,
Letter Sketches, 1880
Van Gogh Museum
Amsterdam, The
Netherlands, Europe

Painted when he was 28.

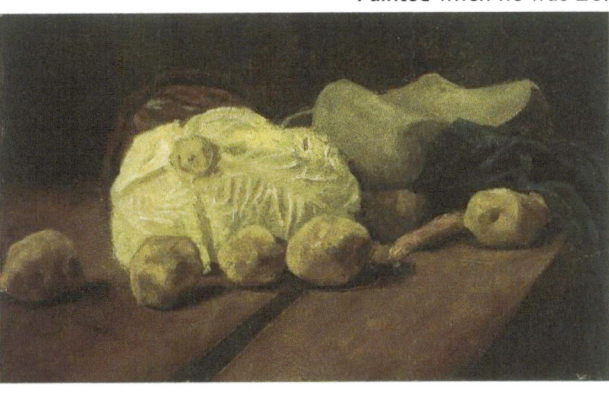

Still Life with Cabbage and Clogs,
Oil on paper on panel
The Hague: 1881
*Van Gogh Museum
Amsterdam, The*
Netherlands, Europe

A few afters...

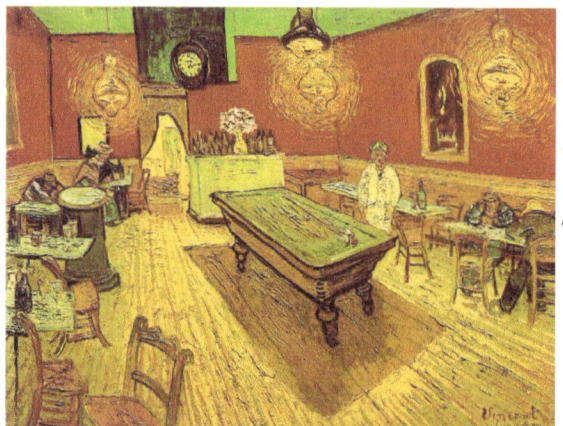

The Night Cafe,
"The Night Café", 1888
Oil on canvas,
Yale University Art Gallery

Painted when he was 35.

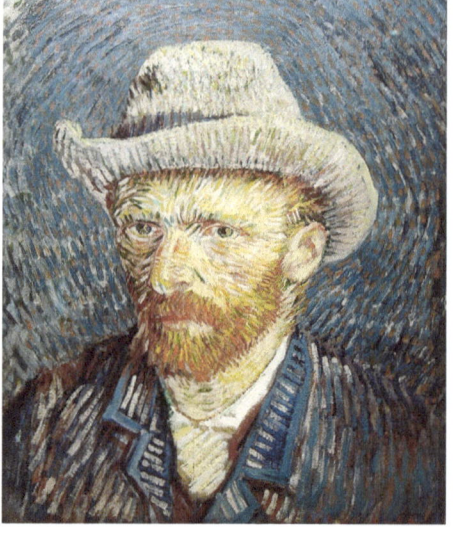

Painted when he was 34.

Self Portrait,
Winter 1887-1888,
Oil on canvas,
Van Gogh Museum, Amsterdam

He has gained a fantastic ability to use colour and emotion in controlled brush strokes. This Dutch Post-Impressionist had an enormous influence on 20th century art, especially on the Fauves and German Expressionists. Van Gogh's paintings now sell for millions all over the world.

What would the world of art look like today has this man decided not to follow his passion to draw and paint?

What can we learn from Cézanne and Van Gogh?

What can we learn from Cézanne and Van Gogh? Let's forget the fact that they both initially had wealthy families who paid their bills. Today, we live like royalty by comparison. Both of these men decided as young men that they wanted to be artists. They weren't children when they decided to be painters. I'm sure they were aware that they had a lot to learn. This may have been to their advantage. They understood the joy they felt when drawing. They focused on learning how to draw and paint. They learned from other artists. Not just any artists either. They learned from the masters! They took those lessons and practiced them until it became second nature. They became THE artist of their time.

I could probably find a ton of art examples on more than just these two artists. The fact is – anything you focus on gets bigger. It's a fact. If you focus on food, you get bigger. If you focus on money, you'll make more. If you focus on learning to draw well, you will become a capable, if not a great artist.

Now you've made the decision to focus on drawing! You've found a teacher here. You're on the right road.

Goals from each student

Ask yourself:

What do you want to draw?

Who are your favourite artists?

Why do you want to draw?

Make a point of writing your answers down. It helps with your though processes!

My goals for You

Drawing is our first language. It's the only thing that truly separated humanity from Neanderthals and it's the one thing that sets us apart from the rest of the animal kingdom. As soon as we're given a crayon or pencil as a child, we draw pictures. We enjoy it. We continue drawing and doodling until people start saying things like, "What's that supposed to be?" and "That doesn't look right." So we stop drawing. We lose the real purpose, which is self expression and enjoyment. People with a natural ability quit too. My own mother quit. She was guilty of telling me "You'll be a starving artist. You'd better get a reliable job. There's nothing wrong with being a cleaner."

Each of us want to draw because it's a pure part of our nature as human beings.

My goal for each of you is to teach you the basics of drawing so that you can draw well. I want you to understand how to use your drawing tools, the most important one being your brain. I want to teach you to ignore what your brain tells you and to draw what you actually see in front of you. Once you've got the basics down you can go and master the art of drawing and move on to trying other things... oil painting, acrylics, water colour, sculpture, etc...

Overview of tools

Paper – medium drawing pad & big drawing pad

Pencils – H stands for Hard (light). HB is the middle ground. Most writing pencils are HB. B is soft (dark).

Other Tools – Sketch sticks, Charcoal sticks, Sharpener, Charcoal Sharpener, Kneaded Eraser (a must), White eraser, Blending stick (stomp), Working fixative (helpful with big drawings you don't want to smudge)

Hands & Eyes – You know where they are I hope! Eyes in head. Hands at ends of arms. Same for most of us! We're going to learn how to use them to draw accurately.

Your Brain – You're going to learn how to turn the one part of your brain OFF that tells you what things look like. Very useful when driving or chewing gum and walking at the same time. Not very useful when drawing.

Exercise 1
(15 minutes)

Lets play with your pencils! Get out your small or medium drawing pad. Scribble a square with each one. Below it, write which pencil lead you're using and scribble, draw lines and cross-hatch in your square. Can you see the difference in value from one pencil lead to another? You don't need to do all of them. Pick a range from H to B - select about 4 or 5 leads. This is just to give you an idea of the tools before you.

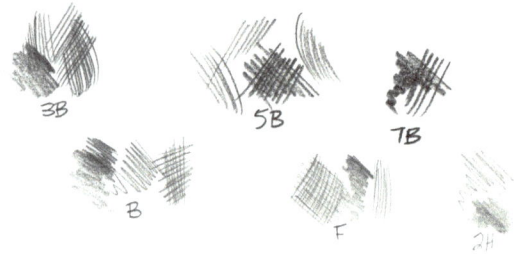

Exercise 2
(30 minutes)

We'll use this piece as your Before in your Before & After – Proof that you learned to draw! So, draw whatever you want. Use objects before you and draw them. Draw something that appeals to you. I'm not instructing you on this one. Just have fun. Shut off your inner editor! Draw

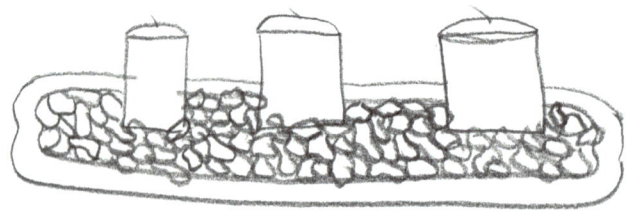

Anyone Can Draw in Ten Sessions

The Elements of Art

Line can be thick or thin, straight or curving, broken, solid, and so forth...

Shape is a flat (two-dimensional), closed space. It's borders are marked by a line (real or imaginary). It can be geometric or organic, big or small.

Value is a spectrum from light to dark. You can create images with a lot of contrast or only a little between black and white (the extremes).

Space is three-dimensional and in a picture (or sculpture) it can be shallow or deep. Space can represent 3-D space in the picture that contains objects or it could mean the "negative" space between objects.

Form is a three-dimensional object and it's often depicted using elements like value and space.

Perspective is something we'll learn about in the next several classes. It's an element in art that helps an artist draw a dimensional object realistically.

Texture is a way of visually representing how something feels to the touch or how you may imagine it to feel.

Colour is fun to experiment with! Try using one or more colours and think about whether and why you want to use bold colours, earth tones, etc. In this drawing workshop we're sticking to pencils - black and white. It is the best place for any budding artist to begin developing the technique and skills needed to become an artist. When designing graphics, the cardinal rule is that designs must first look good in blackand white before they will work in colour.

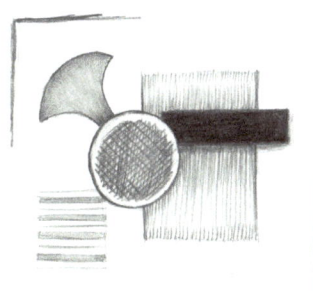

Exercise 3
(30 minutes)

You're going to warm up by experimenting with the elements of art and seeing how many different types of lines, shapes and textures you can draw. Any drawing or painting, whether it's realistic or abstract, uses basic elements in a variety of ways. For this exercise your drawing will be abstract. You're drawing whatever shapes or objects that come to mind.

Use your pencils and charcoal: every medium looks and works differently.

You've also got your Kneadable eraser! Try cross hatching your lines on your page and run your eraser through it. Knead it until you've got a small size and erase something. You'll find this little guy to be one of your favourite tools when you've got a tight spot to clean up on your page. Use your Blending Stomp on at least a portion of your drawing. Go ahead! Smudge something.

Exercise 4

(30 minutes)

Continue experimenting with different ways of representing the elements of art. Draw to music and use abstract art to visually express the rhythm and mood that you hear. This is as much for fun as it is to get you accustomed to using your new drawing tools.

Perhaps the next time you sit down to draw from life or still life, think about how you can use abstraction to represent how you feel about what you're drawing.

Write down what music you listened to while drawing.

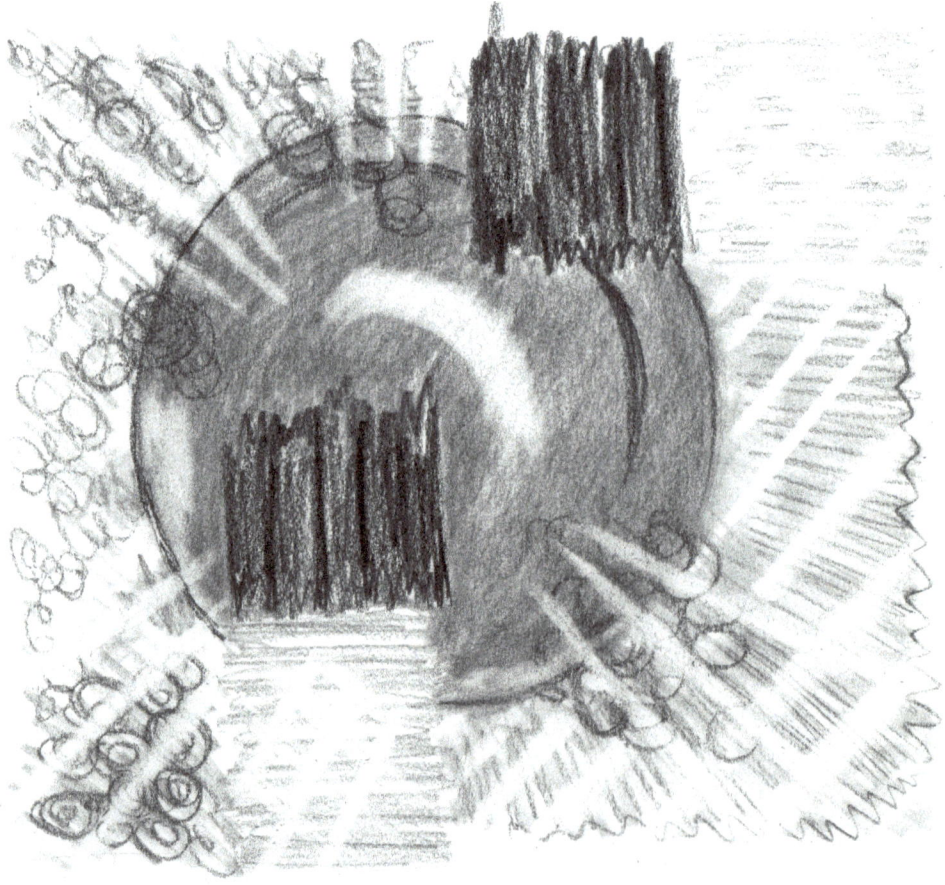

To see a demonstration on using Drawing Tools:
http://www.**youtube**.com/**LindaLaforgeArt**

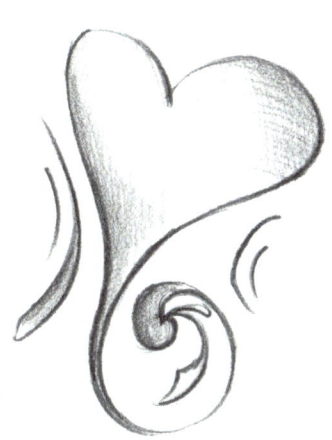

Warm-up Exercise

(10 minute Draw)

Draw anything while thinking of your Valentine. If you don't have one, think of your Dream Valentine.

In this Session we're focusing on:
• How your Brain has been messing up your Drawing
• Holding your pencil
• Directional strokes
• Drawing your own personal Icons
• An intro to Perspective

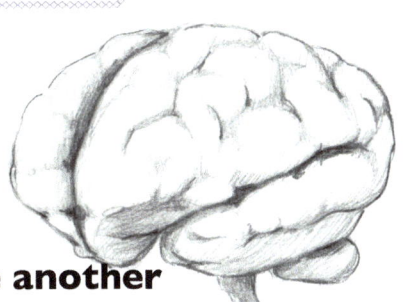

Your Brain is Messing Up Your Drawing!

Brain Work - our info processes at war with one another

Your brain processes visual information in two ways: Spatially and Intellectually

Spatial Thinking: • Keeps you constantly informed on how space changes around you.

• This keeps you safe.

• You can tell how large things are and their relative locations in reference to your body

Intellectual Thinking: • This is the part of your brain that names things.

• It analyses things.

• An important tool that will get you through the day, but it can mess up your drawing big time!

Your *Intellectual Brain* creates simple visual icons or symbols in your brain. Your brain distorts that info, making drawing very difficult. It tells you what an object is *supposed* to look like. It calls up it's icon from its massive database and generalizes the information to make it easier to store. It focuses on surface and *basic* details and ignores structured forms.

Looking at a box, intellectually you know there are 90 degree angles. You see the different sizes of each panel on the box. So you try to draw them, but it doesn't look right. Hmmmm. Why is that?

Exercise 1

(5 minutes)
Lets all draw a box - a simple box

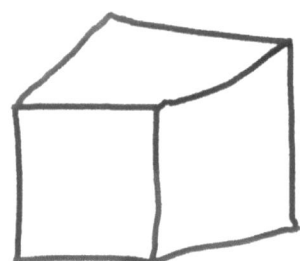

Does your box look a bit like this one? It's not quite right, is it?

Here's the conflict between what you see and what you know.

Perspective - We can see how perspective works. We fight with our brains' "icon" when we draw. If you want to build it, measure the box! *Intellectually*, you'll be able to figure that out. If you can't draw the box, you need to learn how to see the box. You need to learn how to use your *Spatial Brain*.

Your *Intellectual Mind* is messing up your drawing because it's telling you what it thinks the object looks like.

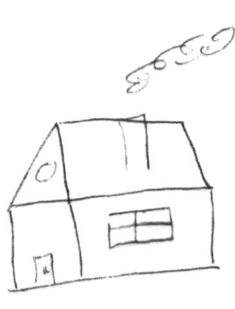

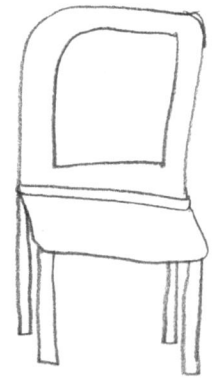

Exercise 2

(15 minutes)
Let's all draw some of our "icon's"

Draw your pet, your house or your car. Draw a few objects. A pine tree, a flower...

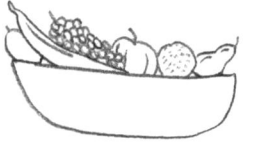

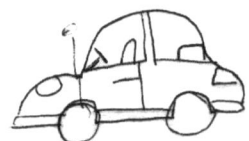

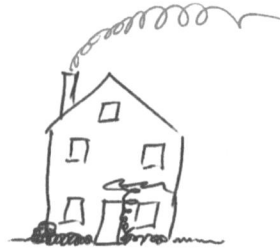

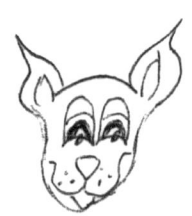

This is what we do as kids. We draw symbols and forms from our own world. We try to make these icons more realistic as we grow up. The ones who are good at that are the ones we call artists. Our *Intellectual Brains* are what our teachers focus on in our school years. That's what we focused on too. So, when we didn't draw well, we got poo-pooed, and we quit.

Anyone Can Draw in Ten Sessions

Sometimes, when we draw, our pictures seem to come from another world. It's the one our *Intellectual Brain* has created with us. If we were taught how to see with our *Spatial Brain* back then, we would all be pretty good Artists if we wanted to be. Instead, we use our own icons to draw, and we keep using those symbols, including the one's we began creating as children. Seeing isn't the same as remembering.

When you prepare to draw something accurately, you need to ignore yourself! Ignore yourself when the voice in your head starts saying, "this is too hard" or "that's too detailed". When you draw an object in detail, adding features, light and contrast, each drawing, even by the same person, will be different.

You're going to learn how to tune out our *Intellectual Thinking* while you're drawing Your *Intellectual Brain* is not creative. **Your intellect cannot draw.**

Your artist's brain

Before you can find freedom as an artist, you need to learn the discipline. As an Athlete develops technique, skill and speed through practicing a series of exercises that teach their body and mind, so will you. We're going to practice through a myriad of exercises too! Each is designed to teach our brains how to see and our hands how to draw what we see.

Our tools
• Spatial thinking
• The ability to see angles
• The ability to see size
• The ability to see position in space
• The ability to see light and dark values (the toughest to put on paper)

Angles
Have you ever put a picture on the wall? Did you compare the top of the picture frame to a door frame or ceiling?
We compare angles in space every day. It's a natural ability. It's an Artists ability!

Size
Are you looking for space when you're looking for a spot to park your car?
When you look at a person, can you tell if his ears are too big or too small?

What about if his lips are too big? I'm thinking Mick Jagger here.
Or maybe you can tell if he or she is just right!
We will use this ability to see and understand what we draw.

Position in space

Have you ever used these words to describe something - "It's about this high?"
When we draw, we map key points as they relate to one another. It's a 3D version of
a road map.
Vertical and horizontal.
You'll use a technique called mapping a great deal.

Value

Did you ever chase your shadow as a kid? We see shapes and objects because of how
the light reflects upon an object and because of the shadow given by that object.
We distinguish forms by the severity or softness of a shadow. This is a skill that takes
time to develop as an artist

Holding Your Pencil

There are myths about
how an artist should hold a
pencil - kinda like the one
that tell us that artists have
long fingers! Never try to
force yourself to use an artificial
grip. That's the worst thing
you can do to your drawing.
It creates needless stress and
upsets the natural flow of your
line work.

The most common way to
hold a pencil is the basic tripod
grip. The basic tripod grip is the
same as the one you probably
use for writing.

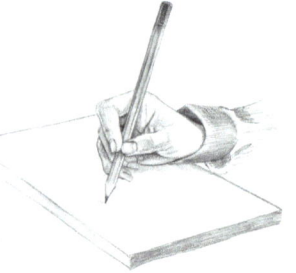

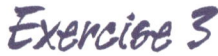

Exercise 3

(10 minutes)

Angle and Direction of Lines – <u>Rulers Not Allowed</u>

We're going to discover your best angle to draw a straight
line. Then, all you have to do is turn the paper to create
a horizontal, vertical, or diagonal line. Right now we're
searching for your favourite direction to draw straight
lines. It's not important which direction you move to get
your straight line - spontaneity and directness is what
really matters. Be brave! Thrash them down in one stroke,
or in several. Have some fun! You're not being tested and
you cannot fail. Relax. Let yourself go. If you can draw a
straight line in any direction without turning the paper
you're special.

Anyone Can Draw in Ten Sessions

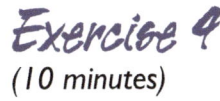

Exercise 4
(10 minutes)

Drawing Basic Shapes

Drawing basic forms helps you learn to see correctly. As you look at an object, no matter how complicated it may seem, the first step is to reduce it to its basic shape. Once you learn how to see, you'll be able to draw the object correctly. Does that make sense?

The basic shapes, forms or models are cubes, cylinders, spheres, hexagons, cones, hemispheres, and pyramids. Draw these shapes on paper and keep on drawing them.

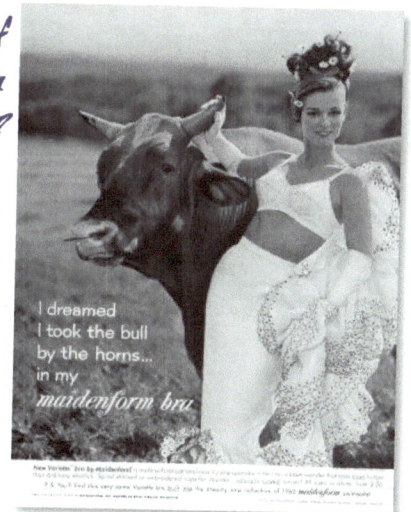

Recognize any of your shapes in this photo?

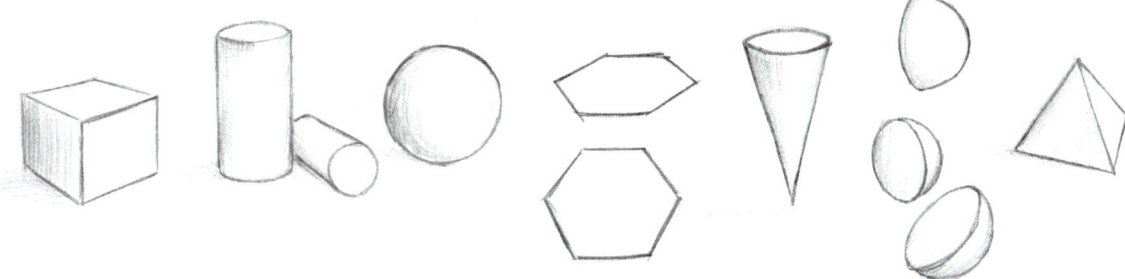

Perspective – intro

Look at the images below. This should help you see how perspective works.

The Horizon Line

The purple line is the Horizon Line. It represents the viewer's eye level. You can see the top of an object if it is below eye level, below the Horizon Line. If an object is above eye level, above the Horizon Line, you cannot see the top.

What's Up?

The red box is above the Horizon Line. See the bottom of the red box?
The blue box is below the Horizon Line. See the top of the blue box?

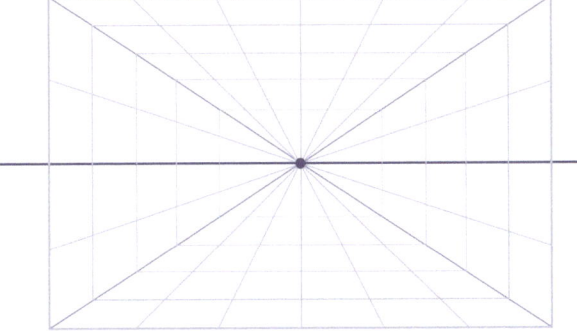

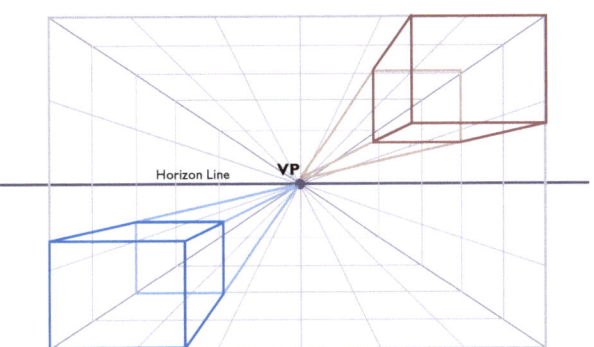

Exercise 5

(30 minutes)

You CAN use a ruler in this exercise. Draw a line in the middle of your drawing page using an H pencil (so it's light). Make sure your page is on a landscape orientation and that your line is drawn in the middle of your page. This is your Horizon Line. Put a dot in the centre of your Horizon Line. This dot represents your Vantage Point or VP. Draw four lines from your VP, each one to a corner of your page. This is a framework to help orient yourself. Now, use a darker pencil to draw a few 3 dimensional boxes. Try some above the Horizon Line too!

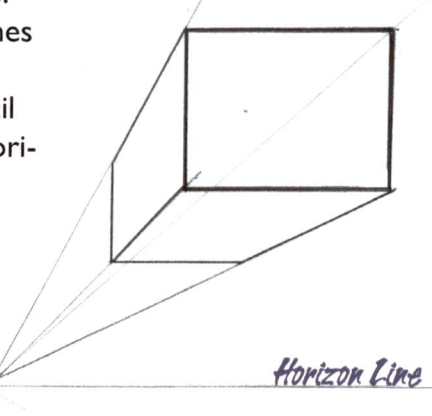

Horizon Line

VP

As you observe your surroundings and identify the basic shapes within the objects you observe, your drawing will improve. You will take this new ability to see shapes as you create new drawings.

Exercise 6

(30 minutes)

Draw boxes! Practice using the Perspective model you just learned. If you get sick of that, try drawing some 'boxy' objects you see everyday. A car, a Kleenex box, your TV...

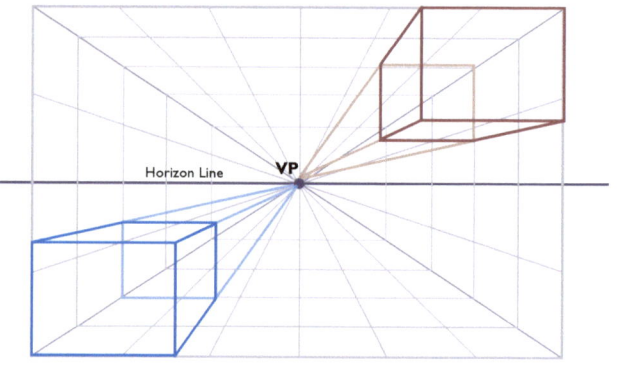

Horizon Line   VP

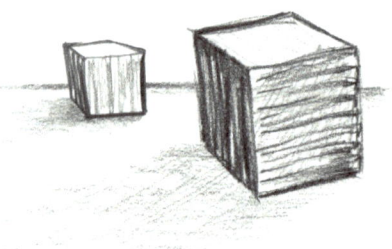

To see a demonstration on how to draw Persepctive visit:
http://www.**youtube**.com/**LindaLaforgeArt**

Warm-up Exercise

(10 minute Draw)

Draw anything while harnessing the feeling of success. Remember the last time you won an award, a game or got a promotion and think of that while you draw a still life object.

> **This Session we're focusing on:**
> • Recap on first Sessions
> • Drawing at your Eye's Speed
> • Drawing Basic Shapes
> • The Planes of an Object
> • More on Perspective

Quick Recap!

Our history lesson...   True or False

1. Paul Cézanne and Vincent Van Gogh were fabulous artists right from childhood! — **True** **False**

2. Cézanne entered the Swiss Academy School of Fine Arts where he learned to draw and paint. — **True** **False**

3. Cézanne actually worked very hard, and hung with and learned from the best; Bazille, Renoir, Monet, Sisley and eventually Manet. — **True** **False**

4. Cézanne became a great artist, and is popular to this day, because he had passion and he worked at developing his skill and creativity as an artist. — **True** **False**

5. Vincent Van Gogh went to a highly reputable school of art in Paris, France. — **True** **False**

6. Van Gogh was a risk taker who was willing to explore new methods of painting with colour and passion. — **True** **False**

7. While he lived in Paris, Van Gogh met and learned from the best; Fernand CORMON, Emile BERNARD & Henri de TOULOUSE-LAUTREC. — **True** **False**

8. Van Gogh created 200 paintings and more than 100 drawings from Feb 1888 to May 1889. — **True** **False**

Answers on page 59

What's the moral to their stories?

Anyone can learn to draw if they really want to, and they put the time into practicing.

Brain work - our info processes at war with one another

Your brain processes visual information in two ways: *Spatially* and *Intellectually*

Spatial Thinking: • Keeps you constantly informed on how space changes around you.
• This keeps you safe.
• You can tell how large things are and their relative locations in reference to your body

Intellectual Thinking: • This is the part of your brain that names things.
• It analyses things.
• An important tool that will get you through the day, but it can mess up your drawing big time!

So, what are we gonna do?
We're going to learn to ignore our *Intellectual Brain* and focus on *Spacial Thinking*.

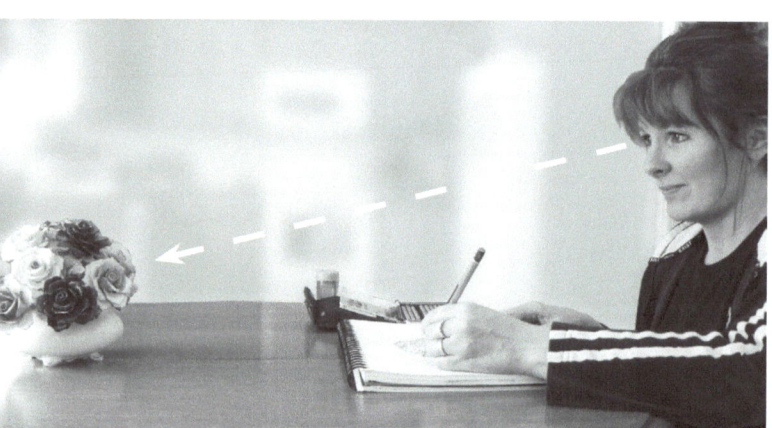

Often our pencils move faster than our eyes can see. The result can be a picture that looks a wee bit like the object we're trying to draw... but it's not accurate. This can be frustrating. The trick is to match the speed of our hand with the speed at which we can see or look at an object. We want to see our object as though we are seeing it for the first time.

Exercise 1
(20 minutes)

Drawing at Eye's Speed

Start drawing at the same speed as your eyes can follow the lines and details in your object. Your pencil has to move across your paper at the same speed as your eyes follow the object. How does that feel? Make sure you can see it clearly. Is there enough light? Is it close enough? Don't worry so much about your drawing as how it feels to truly look at your object and match your pencil speed with your eyesight.

When you get frustrated while drawing, come back to this lesson. It should set you back on your own speed.

Exercise 2
(10 minutes)

Drawing Basic Shapes

Drawing basic forms helps you see correctly. As you look at an object, no matter how complicated it may seem, the first step is to reduce it to its basic shape. Once you learn how to see, you'll be able to draw the object correctly.

We're going to draw the basic shapes again - cubes, cylinders, spheres, hexagons, cones, hemispheres, and pyramids. Draw these shapes on paper and keep on drawing them.

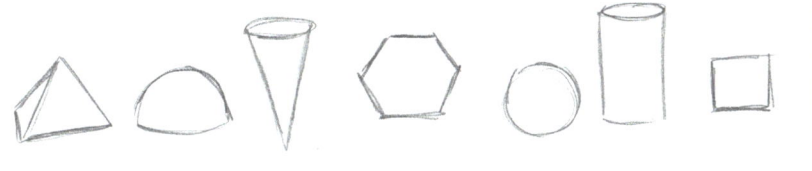

Exercise 3
(10 minutes)

Draw the Outline of a Still Life Object

Use any simple object in our home, like a candle, can or bottle. Forget what you think you see and seek the most basic outlines in your object. An outline is the place where one object starts and another begins. Use something heavy, like a fat marker or charcoal. Feel around the paper. Think how your marks help define the detail of your object.

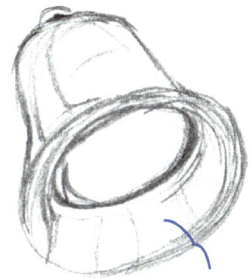

you can erase these construction lines when you're done

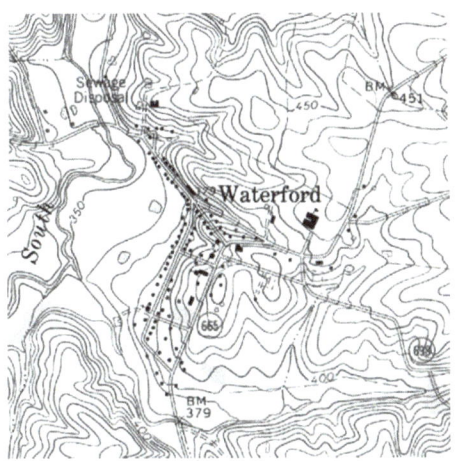

The Planes of an Object

Objects have depth. Within the depth of any object there are other shapes. In a pear, in a plant or a face you will find a myriad of shapes. A topographical map is drawn in this same way. Lines and shadow are used to express peaks and valleys. Artists often draw in this method in their effort to seek a true representation of the object they're drawing. By seeing, and then drawing each shape in relation to the next an artist can create something fairly accurate.

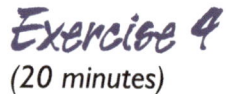

(20 minutes)

See the Planes - (like a topographic map)

We need to pick an object with some serious depth here. A hand. A plant. A piece of fruit. Instead of outlining the one object's shape, you're going to concentrate on the little shapes within the object. Start with either those shapes within the object closer to you, or furthest away. Finish each object with a darker outline and lighter marks representing the shapes within it. Once you've completed one object, go ahead and draw another.

the planes of this apple, drawn lightly

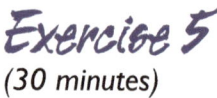

(30 minutes)

Perspective – a repeat and then some

This time we're drawing your shapes using perspective. - cubes, cylinders, spheres, hexagons, cones, hemispheres, and pyramids.

Draw your Horizon line across the centre of your page. Draw your objects in perspective, as shown below.

What's Up?

The red box is above the Horizon Line. See the bottom of the red TV?

The blue box is below the Horizon Line. See the top of the blue TV?

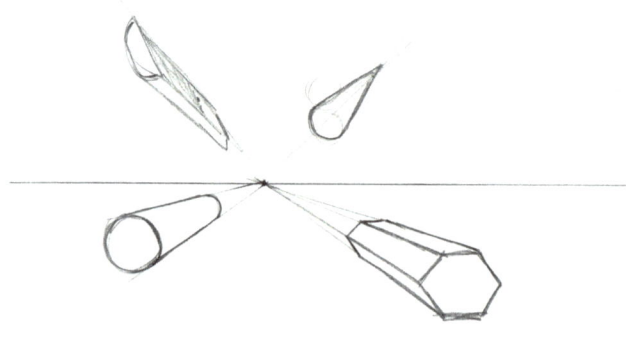

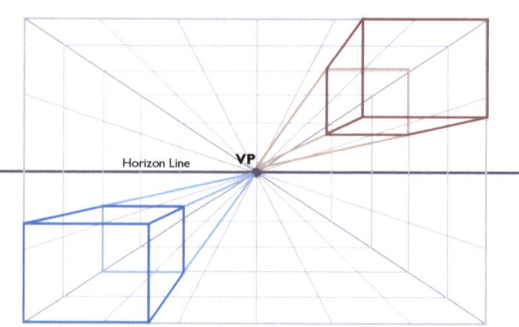

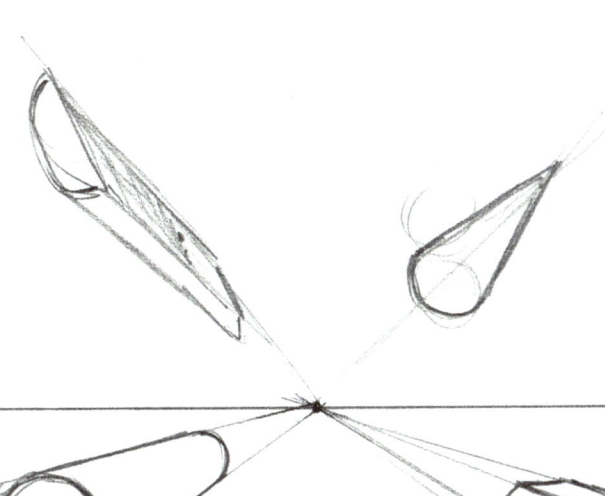

Notice that as an object nears the horizon it's bottom planes get shallower; conversely, as an object drops away from the horizon its top and bottom planes get deeper. Compare the ellipse with that of a cone and a cylinder. Look for this principle in the world about you, even when you're not drawing. This will help when you're ready to sit down and do your homework.

Exercise 6

Practice, Practice! Perspective perfect

Drawing familiar objects using perspective. A bucket, a glass, a car, a book on an odd angle... Use your new ability to understand Perspective to draw your object. This takes practice so don't be upset if it's not perfect right off the bat. Play. Use your Spatial Thinking and ignore that Intellect of yours!

Join the Facebook Group to get feedback and questions answered by the author as well as the group!
https://www.**facebook**.com/groups/114318013917

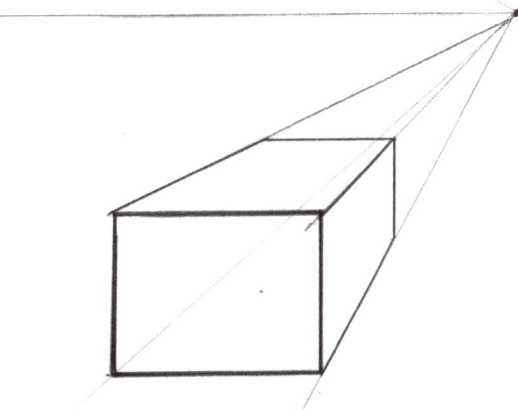

Session Four

Warm-up Exercise

Warm up drawing exercise! Yay!
(Two 5 minute drawings)
1 - Draw using calm, serene marks
2 - Draw using angry marks

> ### This Session we're focusing on:
> • Two Point Perspective
> • The Structure beneath the Objects we Draw
> • Drawing from Still Life

Exercise 1

(45 minutes)

Step by Step - Two Point Perspective

In case you haven't tried drawing two point perspective before, you might think it looks complicated. We'll take it one step at a time.

Note: I call it a Vantage Point when drawing One Point Perspective. To differentiate, and because it's more accurate, we're calling it a Vanishing Point when doing Two Point Perspective. (Don't worry. No test!)

1. Draw your horizon line across the top of your page. Mark two Vanishing Points, as far apart as possible.

2. Draw a short vertical line for the front corner of your box. Now draw a construction line from the top and bottom of the line, to each Vanishing Point (VP).

3. Draw a vertical line to the left of your 'front corner', between the top and bottom construction lines. From the top and bottom points of this line, draw construction lines back to the RIGHT Vanishing Point (VP2). Now, draw a similar vertical line to the right of your 'front corner'. From the top and bottom points

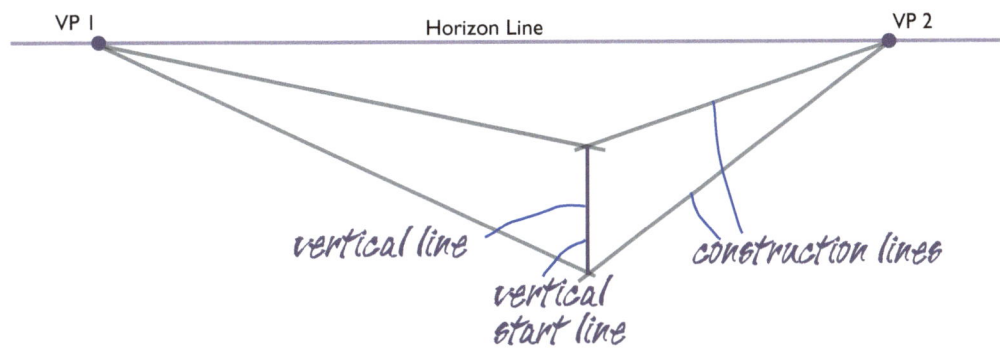

VP 1   Horizon Line   VP 2

vertical line   *construction lines*

vertical start line

of this line, draw construction lines back to the LEFT Vanishing Point (VP1).

4. Where the top construction lines intersect, drop a vertical line to the intersection of the bottom construction lines - this will give you the back corner of the box.

5. Erase the construction lines and any interior lines (unless it's a fish tank!)

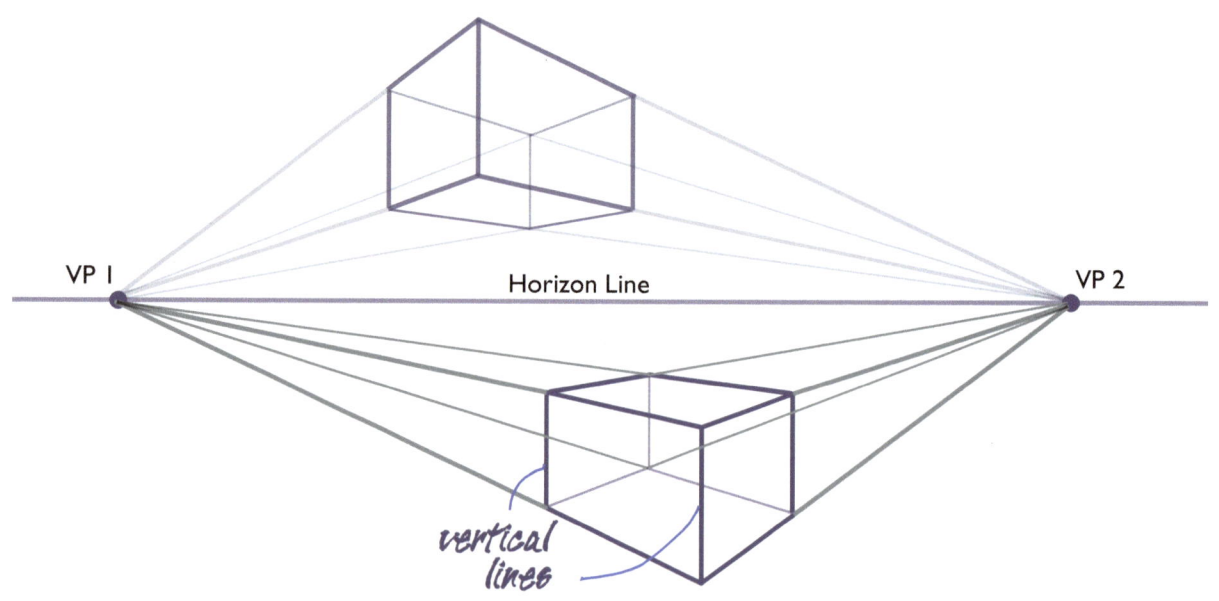

VP 1

Horizon Line

VP 2

vertical lines

Yay! Your first Two Point Perspective Drawing...

Now that you're awesome – keep going! Try using a horizon line at different heights, and placing the box in different places in relation to the Vanishing Points. Note that 'realistic' perspective requires vanishing points that are very far apart - try using a large piece of scrap paper under your drawing paper, and making your vanishing points as far apart as the table (and your ruler) will allow.

To see a demonstration on how to draw Two Point Persepctive visit:
http://www.**youtube**.com/**LindaLaforgeArt**

Anyone Can Draw in Ten Sessions

Exercise 2

(60 minutes)

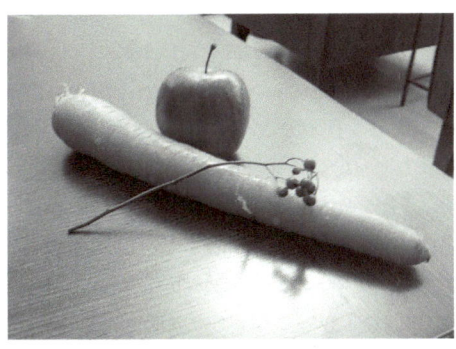

Drawing Multiple Shapes from Life – Using a Pencil to Measure

Find some simple objects to draw. Fruit. Veggies. Some simple ornaments or office accoutrements.

Step by Step – Using a Pencil to Measure

1 Measure the Main Edges

Begin by drawing a line representing one edge of your object. (In this case, I've measured the top and bottom of the carrot) Don't worry about the details. Focus on the *angle* of the whole edge. Hold your pencil out as though placing it flat on a window, keeping one eye closed. Tilt the pencil until it corresponds to the angle of that side of your object. With both eyes, look back and forth from the pencil to your line. Is the pencil at the same angle as the edge of your object? This line is called a *Sight Line*. Correct as you see fit.

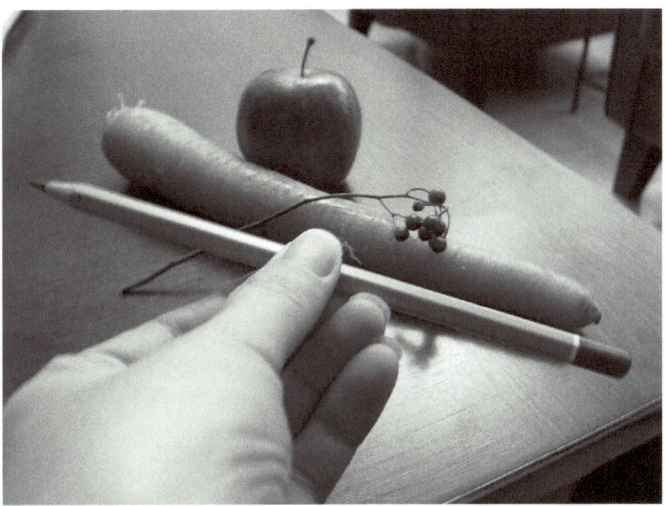

2 Establish Size

The size of your drawing is completely up to you. Your first line determines the size of everything else and the rest will be in relation to this line. Mark where your first angle near the top changes direction and at the bottom where it turns.

Next, add an adjacent angle - the angle along the top edge of the shape. Don't bother with curves or details until you've discovered your angle. Once you establish the direction first, the variations of contour along the angle can be put in with confidence. Look at the angle of the right side. Visualize it already drawn. Now draw it! Hold up your pencil along that angle. Look at your pencil's angle, look at your line, and adjust as necessary. The most important is the angle and size. These lines should be your next *Sight Line*.

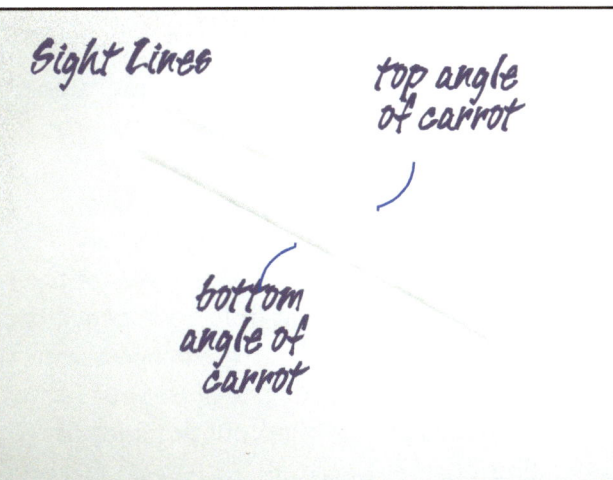

Sight Lines

top angle of carrot

bottom angle of carrot

3 Find the Size Relationship

It's absolutely necessary to keep your arm extended and locked into place while establishing the size of your object, especially if you plan on drawing more than one. Any change in the distance between your pencil and your eye will invalidate your comparison. Place the tip of your pencil at the point where the angle of the top edge changes direction or curves.

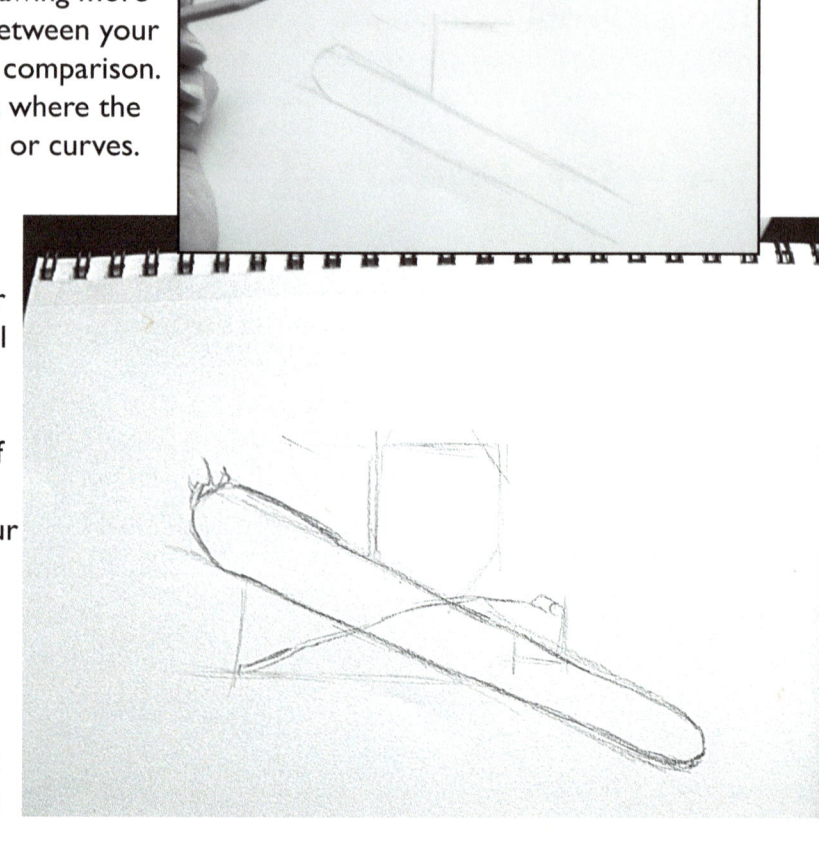

4 Compare Sizes

Keep your arm rigid while you use your thumb to mark the length on your pencil. Rotate your hand until the pencil is parallel to the left side and the tip of your thumb is at the bottom of the first line you drew. See where the tip of your pencil comes to on your object? Move your pencil up until the tip of your thumb is at that point. Note where the tip of the pencil comes again and move your thumb up to that point.

5 Correct the Size Relationship

Go to your drawing and divide the first line you drew, the one representing the left side, into thirds. You now know the length of the top angle. You're using the pencil to get the same size relationship in your drawing. It's not an actual measurement – it's a comparison.

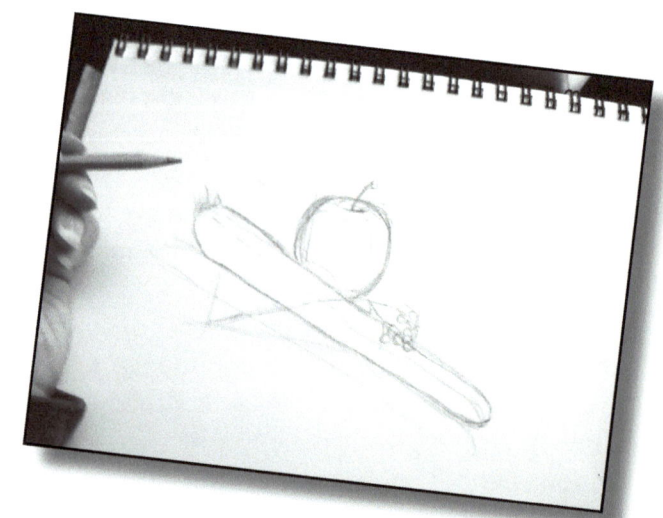

6 Check Sizes and Angles

Use your pencil to see the angles of the right. Draw your line, then hold your pencil back up to the subject and repeat the process, looking back and forth from your pencil to your drawn line. When you're satisfied, check its length with the first edge.

To see a demonstration on Measuring see the Harry Potter Drawing at:
http://www.**youtube**.com/**LindaLaforgeArt**

7 Find Positional relationship

When you complete the shape, your rough drawing contains the essential elements - the proper width to height, the tilt of your shape and the way it sits on the surface of your page.

8 Add Sight line

Hold your pencil horizontally and bring it up until it's touching the widest point on the right side of your paper. Sight along the pencil and see what's on the left side. Is there an object there to add to your drawing? Go to the right and do the same. Draw *Sight Lines* where needed. It'll be helpful in refining your shapes.

9 Refine your shape

Round out the curves where your general angles meet. Can you see how important the angles are? The curves fall into place if the angles are right.

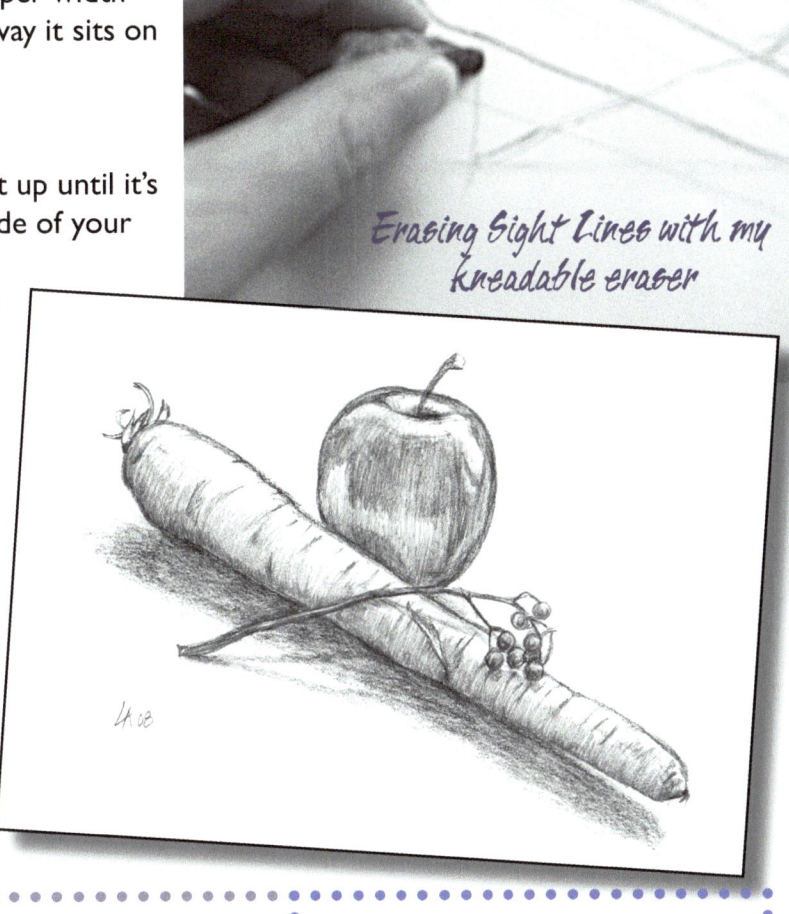

Erasing Sight Lines with my kneadable eraser

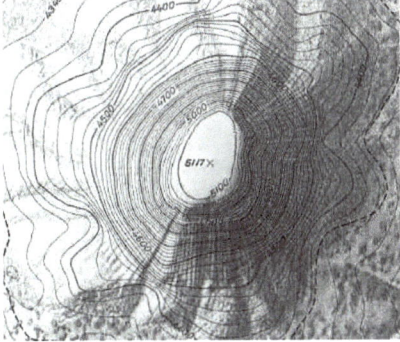

Exercise 3

(60 minutes)

Draw a few objects in Two Point Perspective. Don't worry too much about shading yet. Draw the objects in an outline, drawing all of the shapes within your object with lighter lines.

Life Lesson! For most of my years as an artist, I drew and added value and shading as I went, rather than mapping out my entire drawing using shapes. After much time and effort, I would find that I drew an eye out of line or a nose too long, Once the value is added it's much more difficult to fix! Being introduced to this methodical way of drawing, there was a vast difference in the quality of my work. Learning this took me quickly from competent novice to technically skilled and masterful. I only wished I had learned it earlier!

Warm-up Exercise

Warm up drawing exercise! Woot woot....
Two 5 minute drawings

1 - draw a single object feeling peaceful and serene
2 - draw a single object thinking you are ebeing inundated with conflicting inner voices

> ### This Session we're focusing on:
> • Drawing from Life - Contour Line Drawing
> • Drawing Multiple Objects
> • Drawing using all your new tools

Contour line drawing

The essence of line

In nature we don't see lines. We see the edges of shapes. Artists use lines to describe these edges on a flat surface. Apart from its role in describing edges, the line has character of its own. It can be bold or delicate, energetic or graceful. Lines are expressive of both of the subject drawn on paper and of the person who drew it.

Most beginning artists are afraid to put a line down. Most seem to believe they'll minimize errors if they commit to putting down lots of short lines. Those drawings can look sketchy and unsure. If drawing a fur ball, this is effective, but when drawing solid objects with clearly defined edges, these lines look hesitant and timid. Practicing contour line drawing will develop your confidence. Your lines need to be deliberate and correct and can become so beautiful.

Be confident

Even if the shape is accurate, the lines say more about the artist's hesitation than they do about the edge of the object. Your goal is to suggest the fullness of an object's form. Each line needs to appear deliberate, as if placed exactly where intended. Even if the shape is a bit inaccurate, we assume it's right because of the sureness of the lines. (You know people like that don't you? They act confident, but are they?)

Express mood and energy

Pay attention to the energy behind each stroke. Flowing lines convey a graceful movement. Lines can be explosive, like a bolt of electricity or they can be soft and delicate. Imagine a variety of subjects those lines can express.

What is contour?

Contour moves with the edge of a form, defining where a plane changes direction, or where one part overlaps another. It's not confined solely to the edge where shape meets space, but often move into the interior of the form. An outline, however, is the outside edge of the form, the edge that would be defined in a silhouette.

Organic shapes are excellent subjects for contour line drawing because they have edges or contours that overlap and move from the outer edge into the interior.

Silhouette - A silhouette defines where the entire form meets space.

Outline - Like the silhouette, outline only defines the outside edge of the form.

Contour Line - Contour lines follow the edges of the forms as they move through space. The lines are sharp and crisp, just like the brittle edges of leaves on a plant.

silhouette

outline —

A contour line drawing. Notice the lines have different weights and character?

Point-to-Point Contour

Contour line drawing is a slower, more deliberate kind of drawing that emphasizes hand eye coordination and a feeling for the forms or objects drawn.

Exercise 1
(15 minutes)

Place the tip of your pencil on any point of your paper where a contour will begin. Then, look at the subject to determine the point where the contour changes direction or overlaps another contour. Picture that point on your paper, then pull the pencil line along the contour, matching each bump and change with a corresponding shift in the line. Pause when you reach the point. When the pencil is still in contact with the paper, find the next point and continue your contour. Lift your pencil only when you reach the end of the contour.

Exercise 2
(15 minutes)

Drawing using Contour Lines

Tape down a piece of paper so it won't move. Low tack tape is great for this! Place a random number of dots on the page. Then, using a 4B or 6B pencil held only between thumb and forefinger, pull a line between two of the dots, pause, locate the next point and pull the line to that point. Try varying the line between points by twisting your pencil as it moves, or changing the pressure. Don't hold the pencil as if you were writing and don't use the typical 'Tripod Grip' shown in Session One. Writing is composed of short lines created by the movement of the fingers. You want longer, more fluid lines created by the movement of your whole arm. Draw from your shoulder.

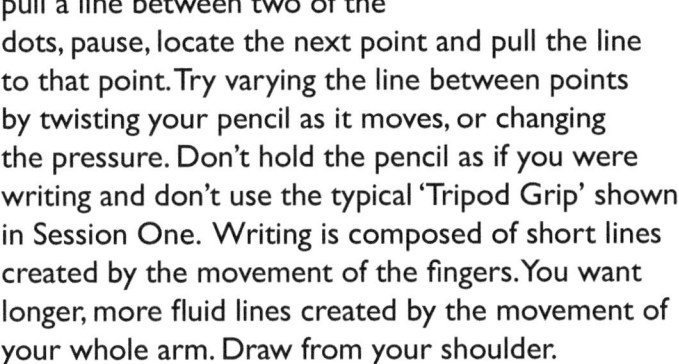

Exercise 3
(40 minutes)

Practice your Line

Focus on *Line Work* and putting your body into your drawing. Try to draw objects accurately, even though that's not THE point of this particular exercise. Start out by measuring, using Sight Lines as before using a Hard Lead, light pencil.

Now add your contour lines. Absolutely NO SHADING! You're striving for beauty of line. Use your arm instead of your fingertips. You use your whole body when you dance, not just your feet. The same is true here. Practice pulling lines with sudden changes in the line density. Discover the line varieties that are possible by twisting the pencil, laying it down to pull sideways, and pressing down to pull the tip. Emphasize the point of directional change with a slightlly heavier pressure or lighter pressure.

You're going to draw a group of objects. A number of subjects are good for contour drawing. Organic objects usually provide a lot of contours and make an interesting drawing. Eggbeaters, tools, and toys make excellent subjects, as does twisted wood and old shoes. Go thick where your object looks or feels thick. Go thin where it looks or feels fine or dainty.

I use line thoughtfully, with flourishes and thin to thick lines when I design my Celtic Knots. You should find this a very enjoyable exercise.

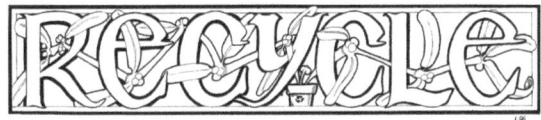

Using Line to Explain Form

Folds of Fabric

Clothing make an excellent subject for contour line studies because it has edges that begin in the interior, move to the exterior, then disappear behind another fold. See the planes, as you would on a topographic map. That's sort of what we're creating when we draw contours!

Points to Remember

- Be confident.

- Imagine your pencil point is in contact with the contour of the subject.

- Go slow. Don't let your eye get ahead of your line. Draw at your eye's speed.

- Let the movement come from your arm.

- Try not to lift your pencil until you've reached the end of your contour.

- Erasing intensifies error.

Exercise 4
(30 minutes)

Draw the material in the image below or set up some of your own. Draw your contours without allowing your pencil to leave the page. This doesn't need to be a perfect drawing. The exercise here is to start your drawing by measuring the shapes and angles and size them on your page. Draw the shape outlines lightly and then add the contours with a darker, softer lead. By teaching your eyes and hand to work together you'll be able to draw anything. Remember to draw at your Eye's Speed, so work at a pace that is natural to you and seek all the little shapes within the fabric.

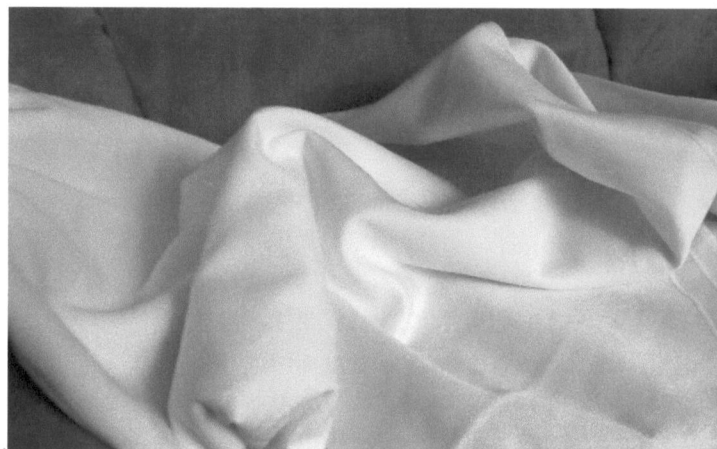

Exercise 5

(30 minutes)

Challenge yourself - Subjects like a twisted piece of wood or trees are excellent because contours emerge only to disappear behind other contours. Outside edges become inside contours. Some outside contours move through the form and emerge on the opposite side. Find a tree or twisted piece of wood, or a plant or something as close to this as you can and draw it. Include all of it's contours!

This time you can let your pencil leave the page when it feels right!

Key! Visualize your subject as a drawing. You don't have to see all the details, but translate it to your object or objects into a drawing. What will it look like?

You want an overall object that will help relate all of your shapes.

Anyone Can Draw in Ten Sessions

Session Six

Warm-up Exercise

Warm up drawing exercise! Have fun... let loose.
(Two 5 minute drawings)
1 - draw using only straight lines
2 - draw making only circles

> ## This Session we're focusing on:
> • The Structure of Objects and Living Things
> • Light Source & Value
> • Drawing from Still Life

the Bones of the Thing

An object has structure, as we humans have bones and organs beneath our skin. One of the creepiest things artist like Leonardo D'Vinci did – he illustrated dead bodies. He even pulled their skin back to see their internal structure. (He was as much a man of science for his time as he was an artist. I love that guy!) He wanted to know why we look and move as we do so he could 'imitate' them on canvas more accurately.

These days Cadavers refrigerated and pickled in formaldehyde are awful. Consider Renaissance Italy, the early 1500's; Leonardo had creepy midnight vigils with the local corpses, without all the good stuff. He had to work quickly. In his own words, "living through the night hours in the company of quartered and flayed corpses fearful to behold." It must have stunk to high heavan!

Creepy, but brilliant. Lucky for us, Leonardo and others have already done the gross stuff for us.

From Wikipedia on Leonardo D'Vinci

"Renaissance humanism saw no mutually exclusive polarities between the sciences and the arts, and Leonardo's studies in science and engineering are as impressive and innovative as his artistic work,

recorded in notebooks comprising some 13,000 pages of notes and drawings, which fuse art and natural philosophy (the forerunner of modern science). These notes were made and maintained daily throughout Leonardo's life and travels, as he made continual observations of the world around him."

Understanding the structure of an object or living thing is paramount when drawing accurately. It helps us keep our subject proportionate and believable.

Exercise 1
(5 minutes)

Value – Shading & Light Source
We're going to start with a simple exercise and work into it. Take each one of your pencils out, one at a time. I've got a sheet of paper with boxes printed on it (found on page 60). You're going to use your H2 and work your way over to your B6. With each one you're going to fill in your boxes, shading light to as dark as you can get. Then you're going to do it one more time, but with crosshatching – just to give you a feel for texture. Make sure you match your pencil with the right title!

We're doing this so that you know the **full range** of your tools – so you know just how light and just how dark you can get when adding value (shading) to your drawings. This should help a lot with your next still life

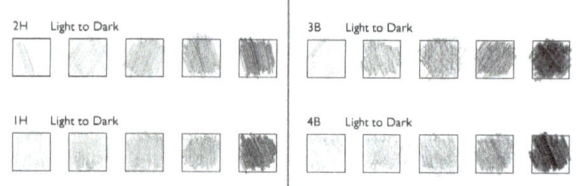

Exercise 2
(5 minutes)

Drawing Basic Shapes – repeat – but not really!
So, draw a cube, a cylinder, a sphere, a hexagon, a cone, a hemisphere & a pyramid in one row. Repeat three more times! Finish with four rows of the same shapes on your page.

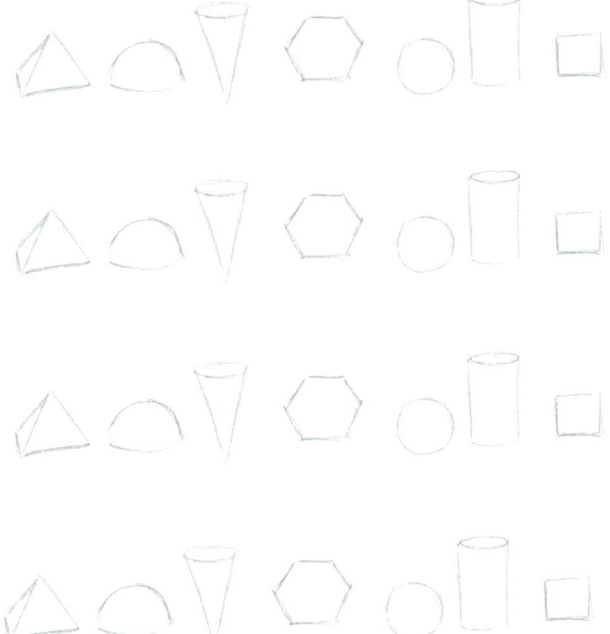

Value
Value is one of the basic elements of drawing. Much like line/shape, perspective, and the big picture (some call this Gestalt) value is creating light and shadow. Balancing the light and dark areas of a drawing is just as important as getting the proportion right.

Shades of Gray
In life as in art, there is black and there is white and all those grays in between. Shading is what allows you to turn a flat piece of paper into a realistic looking portrait, landscape or still life. Variety in gray values make up the lights and shadows that create form, add substance and meaning to shapes, and help develop perspective for the viewer.

Examining your subject, whether from life or photos, guides you in identifying value before you even set pencil to paper.

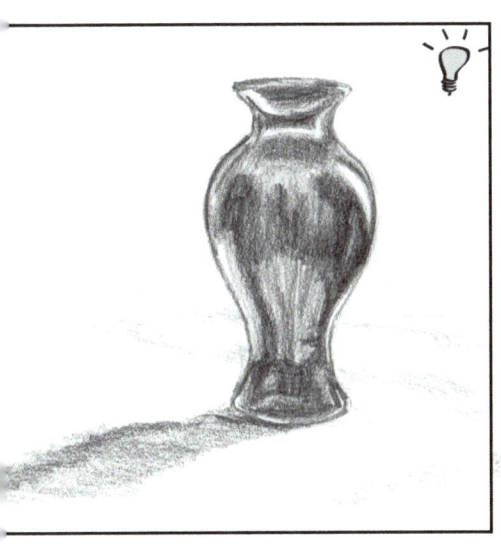
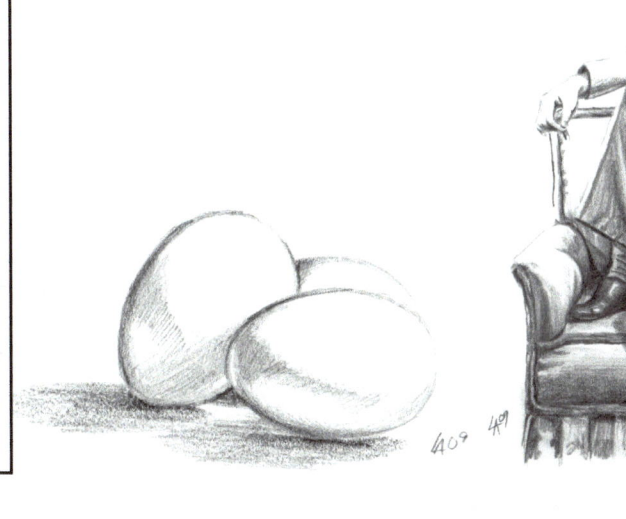
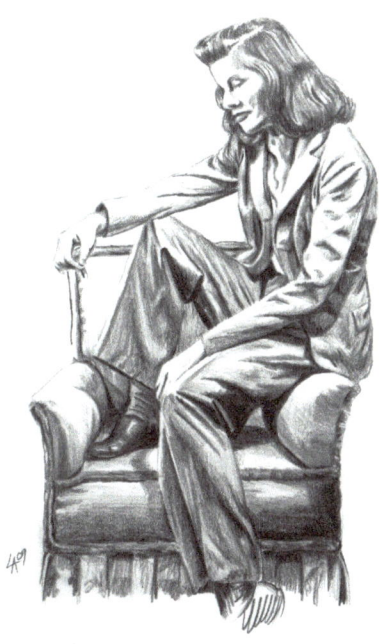

1. Find the light source.
Everything we look at has a light source. The impact of your drawing comes from how sharp or soft your light source is. Hard light sources are often not usually flattering - they don't contribute to creating shadows, like when the camera flash goes off - it flattens people's features by washing them out and removes variety in light and shadow. Side lighting will create enough contrast to bring out the detail in your subject. Back lighting makes your subject dramatic and softer in appearance. (Also makes cool silhouettes.)

2. Find the values.
Now that you know where your light source is, you can start to pick out the values. You will see bright, almost white areas, light values, middle grays, and dark, to black areas. Generally, the shadows created by objects on your subject and shadows cast by your subject will be the middle to dark values. The brighter values are highlights and the light-to-middle values are the areas in between. Highlights also occur when the light source is bouncing off of a reflective surface, like water, metal or eyeballs. The eggs, above, reflect white underneath as well as give off a shadow.

3. Find the relationships between the values.
Most drawings – especially drawings that are going for a realistic look – do not have strong lines between the values. You may notice that when a hard line divides different values, the result appears forced. This is a good technique when you are developing contrast, but when your goal is creating a representational drawing those hard lines should be avoided. The relationships between values can be created with blending (also called tonal value) or drawing yet another value that lies between the two values sitting beside each other.

Exercise 2B
(10 minutes)

Light Source and Shade – the reason we had to draw dumb shapes again!
Add shading to your shapes. Each row of shapes has a completely different light source, as shown to your left. It does take some practice to get it right...

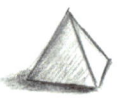

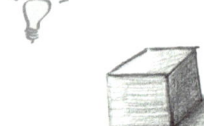

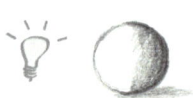

Exercise 3
(10 minutes)

Draw shades of gray in the white material
We're going to draw another lump of white material. If you're at home, use this image as an example of how to lay out your material. There are distinct lines or areas of gray that are much easier to see when you're not influenced by color. You can see the relationships between the values. In this example, there are some hard lines and there are areas of gradation where one value blends into another.

When working from a live subject, squinting helps pick out values.

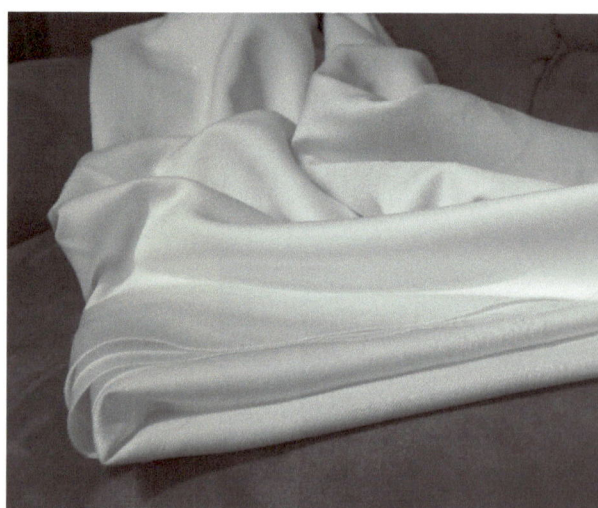

As usual, measure and size your shapes (objects) on your page, lightly outline all of the shapes in the folds of the fabric. Once that's done, then you can start shading... it's almost like 'paint-by-numbers', only with pencils!

Exercise 4

Finding Similar Angles within a Shape
Look for objects that share a similar angle. You should find several. You're going to develop your search muscles. Practice on magazine photos, your own photos, or images you find online (print those ones out). Get in the habit of looking for angle relationship. Draw a few of them! Try adding values of light and dark to them!

Anyone Can Draw in Ten Sessions

Warm-up Exercise

Warm up drawing exercise! Have fun....

(15 minute drawings)

1 - Draw anything using 3 leads, like H, HB & B4. How are you feeling today?
   Put that into your strokes!

> ### This Session we're focusing on:
> • More practice drawing from Life - Grouping Multiple Objects
> • Rough edges to Finished Drawing
> • Drawing using all your new tools

Drawing from Life - grouping multiple objects

Finding the shape of your drawing

Figures can fit so nicely into an equilateral triangle, or any specific shape. Often a complex figure or groups of figures fit perfectly into a rectangle, triangle or square. If some objects don't fit perfectly into a nicely shaped grouping at this stage, don't worry. Often you can move them around until the grouping balances.

New artists often feel compelled to line things up. Ignore that desire. Grouping objects together in ununeven numbers, like 3 or 5 work best.

1. Rough in the Biggest Shapes

We're drawing multiple objects – like the ones below. Create a grouping of objects that appeal to you. It's easier to relate a small shape to a bigger one. So start with your biggest shapes: three objects are a good place to start.

Begin with the vertical lines belonging to your largest shape. Decide how tall you want to make it, and then see how wide it is compared to the height. Where is the top? Now check the length of it adjacent to the next biggest object. Find the width of your largest object and you can block in the contours with *Sight Lines*.

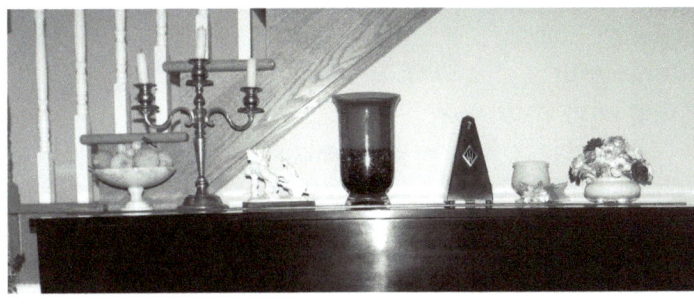

2. Draw Using the Height and Width

How does the length of your object compare to your second, closest object? How does it's height compare. Start drawing in sighting lines of your second object... and then your third (if you choose to draw 3 objects).

3 Refine the Edges

Be exact about what happens along their edges. Look at the shapes of the shadow that defines the forms. Check the relative width of the stems and the spaces between them. <u>Lightly</u> add the contour of your objects.

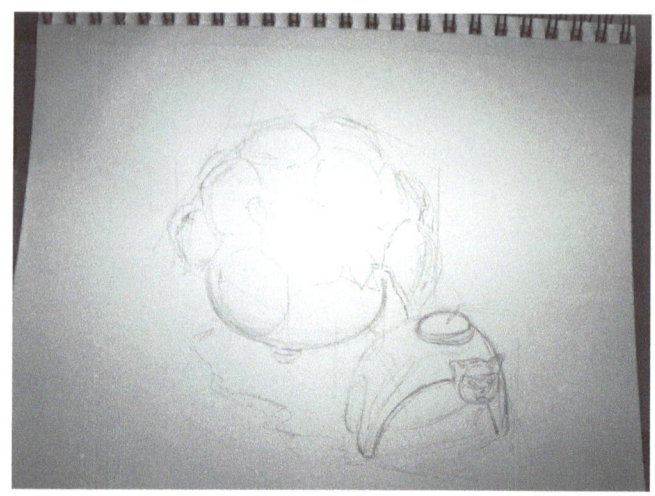

4 Add the Values

Don't be hesitant to put in *Sight Lines*. They aren't present in the subject, yet notice how few of them remain once you start adding value. Some become part of your drawing, and the axis lines often become completely submerged.

This step only involves putting in values. It doesn't involve putting in more details. If you want to lavish attention on something, get the exact configuration of the shape first. I draw those details in lightly with a hard pencil – an H2. Then I pull out softer pencils and begin shading in the values as my last step.

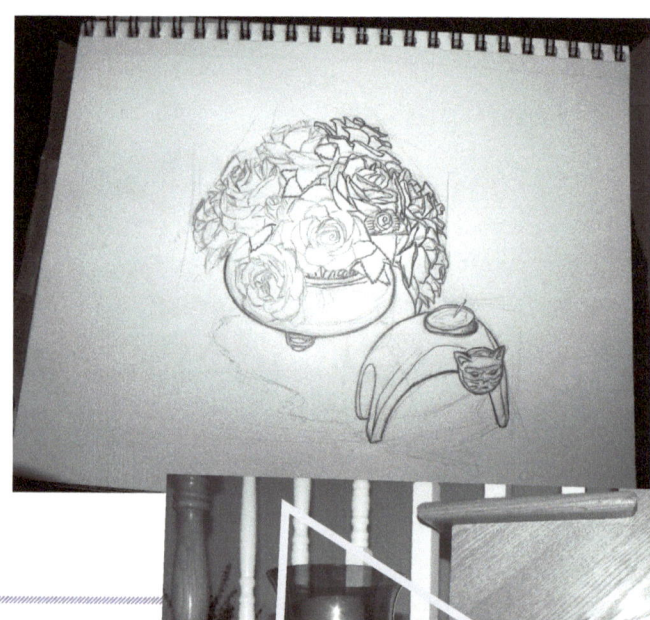

Exercise 1
(2 Hours)

grouping objects in a shape look much better.

Draw three to five objects together. Set-up a grouping of things that you want to draw and create a shape to fit them within like a triangle, a square or a circle. Triangle groupings of three or five often make the best drawings. Use your pencil and arm as a tool to help measure, starting with your largest object. Create *Sight Lines* as needed for each object. Refine your edges once you've got placement. Then draw the contours within each shape and begin adding values. Draw what you see and ignore that *Intellectual Brain*! Be conscious of where your light source is.

don't line them up!

Take your time. Enjoy the challenge before you. Once you've completed your first drawing, change seats and try drawing the same three objects from a new vantage point. Try three more objects!

Exercise 2

Draw three of your favourite things together! Maybe it's a bucket of ice cream and a pop? Maybe it's your cat sleeping on your couch, on your favourite pillow? Anything. Anyone. Draw it from a photo or from life. Start with your rough drawing and complete it by adding value through shading. Don't forget to have fun! When you get frustrated, get up and do something silly to make yourself smile. (It works!)

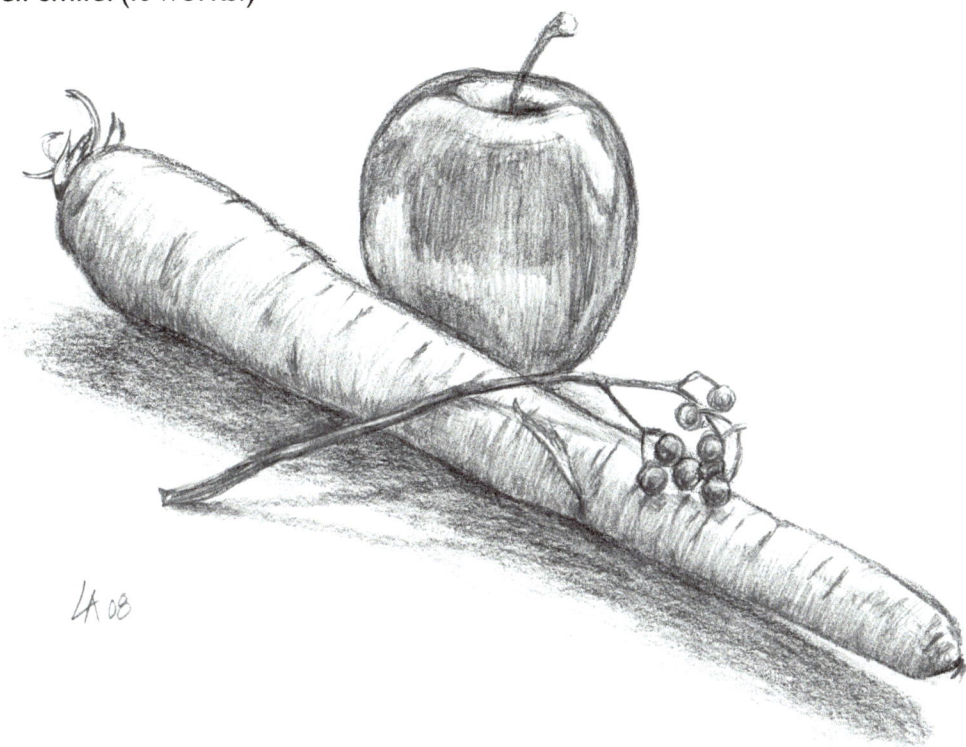

Note: Next Session involves working with a photo of the face of someone you'd like to draw. Make sure it's sharp and clear.

Drawing Position

When drawing, an artist must look directly upon the page in order to create accurately proportionate work.

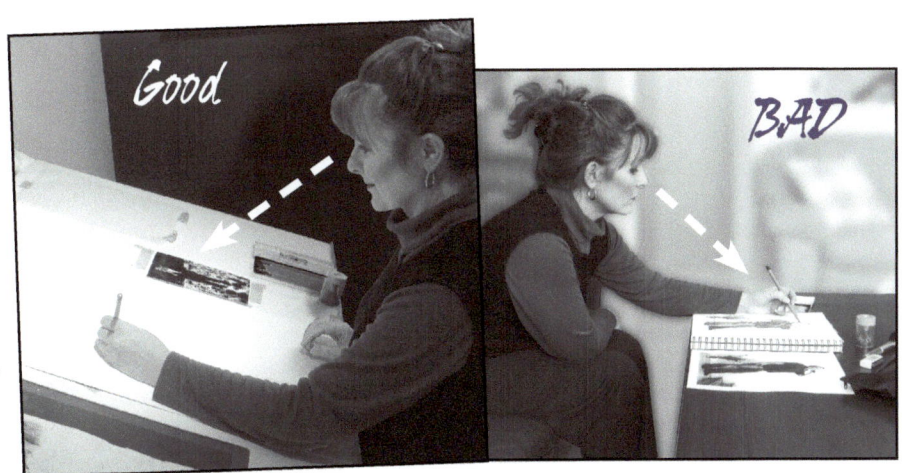

Warm-up Exercise

Warm up drawing exercise! Yeeeee ha....
Two 5 minute drawings

1 - draw using one unending line
2 - draw using only dots (ink is best for this one)

This Session we're focusing on:
- How to Draw People - Faces
- Drawing using all your new tools

Capturing a Figure

When I ask workshop students what the most challenging subject is, the most common answer, by far, is People. As children, we develop an extensive repertoire of symbols about people. Later, when we attempt to draw them, the symbols become substituted in place of observation. Even though we are very familiar with the figure, we never had to draw one. In order to reconstruct it, we need to forget about the hair, nose, etc., and focus on shapes and their relationships.

We want to remind ourselves of our previous lessons. First, ignore your Intellectual Brain. ◉< THIS is NOT what your subject's eye really looks like. Go through the same full process of drawing, using the steps you've learned. See all of the shapes in the face and draw what you see.

Grab your photo. It's time to draw!

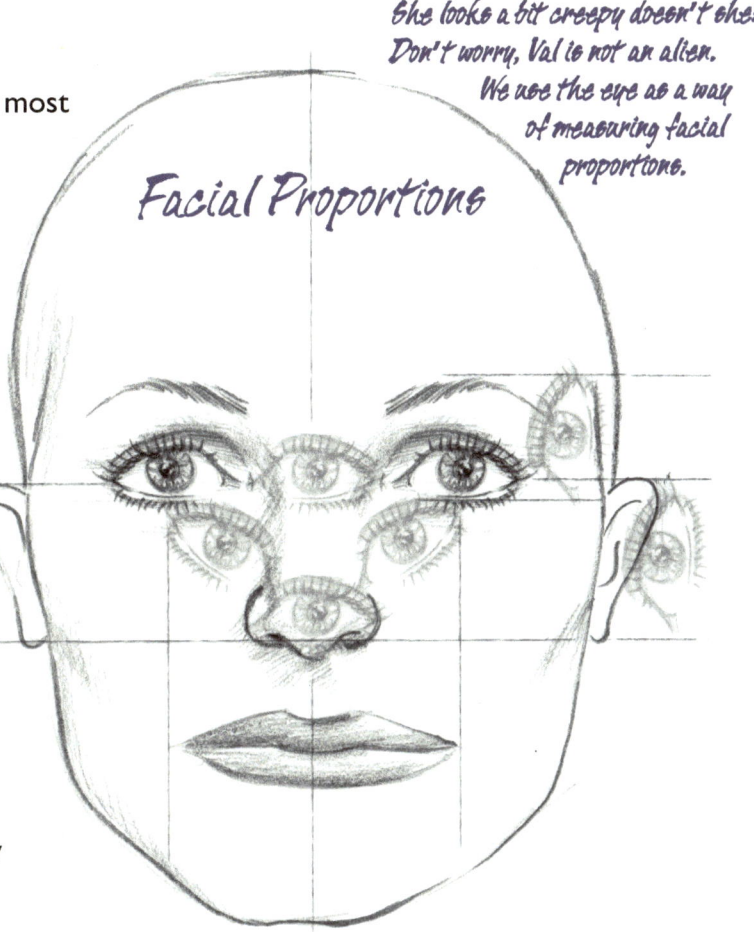

She looks a bit creepy doesn't she? Don't worry, Val is not an alien. We use the eye as a way of measuring facial proportions.

Facial Proportions

Exercise 1

(2 hours – it's a pretty worthy challenge!)
Tape down your photo, as shown.

1 Begin Your Search

Begin your search with a simple vertical line, to represent the centre and angle of the face. This helps you find the correct tilt of the head. We're seeking an angle relationship to your vertical line next – so draw a *Sight Line* on the angle of your person's head.

Follow with *Sight Lines* for the angles of the eyes and mouth. Then set up the width and height of the head, which will become the size comparison for everything else.

This stage in the search is about getting the right tilt or angle to the shapes, locating landmark points and getting the correct sizes. It is not about eyeballs, wrinkles or details.

Finding the Angles & Measuring using the Pencil

2 Refine the Shapes

This second step is like the first - a search for the relationships of shapes. The only difference is now you narrow the search to smaller shapes within the large chunky shapes you developed in step one. The emphasis is not on final appearance but on drawing shapes at the right size, set at the right angle and in the right place.

Here's where new artists often mess up. Your *Intellectual Brain* wants to take over. It wants you to draw what it thinks an eye or a nose or a mouth

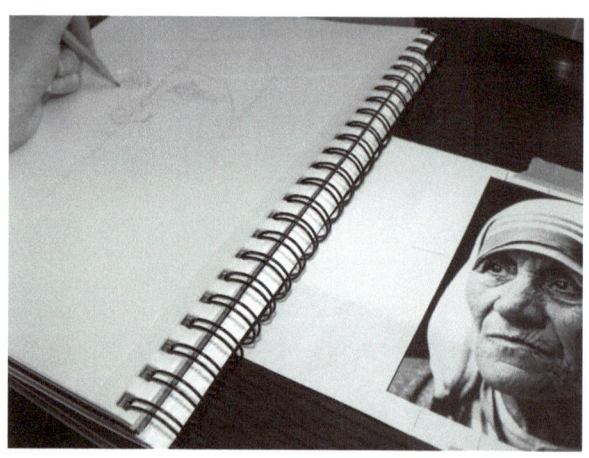

looks like. Remember – your *Intellectual Brain* can't draw! Use your *Spacial Thinking*. LOOK at your photo closely. How does each shape and little curve relate to the next?

3 The Final Stage

Focus on what the drawing is about – a drawing. Try to make the values in each area right. As you move further from this focal area, ask yourself if certain shapes need more detail to make the drawing complete. Keeping light and dark values offer a sense of space and location so don't be afraid of contrast.

Leave the *Sight Lines* if you like - they are part of the process. A drawing has it's own life. In the end, it has to live as a drawing, not as an exact copy of the photo. These lines are a personal part of the artist's, your, response and are as much part of the drawing as anything.

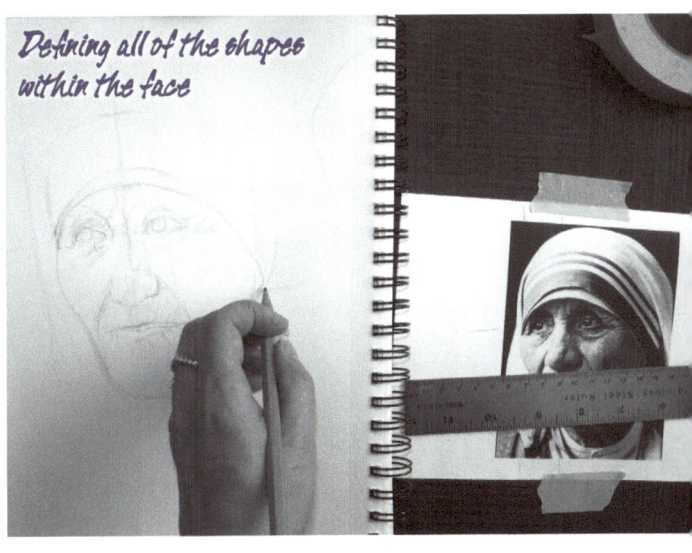

Defining all of the shapes within the face

KEY: If you're having trouble seeing what's actually in the photo, turn it upside down and draw it upside down. It turns your Intellectual Thinking off!

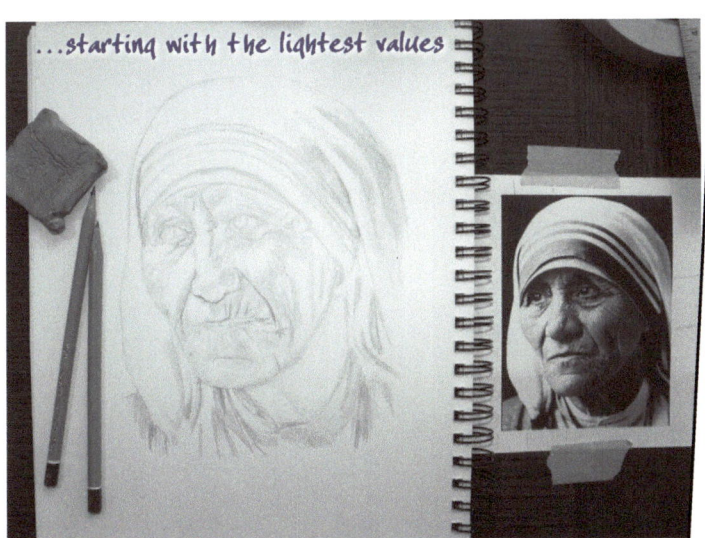

...starting with the lightest values

KEY: Whether drawing or painting, I always start with the lightest values and work towards the darkest.

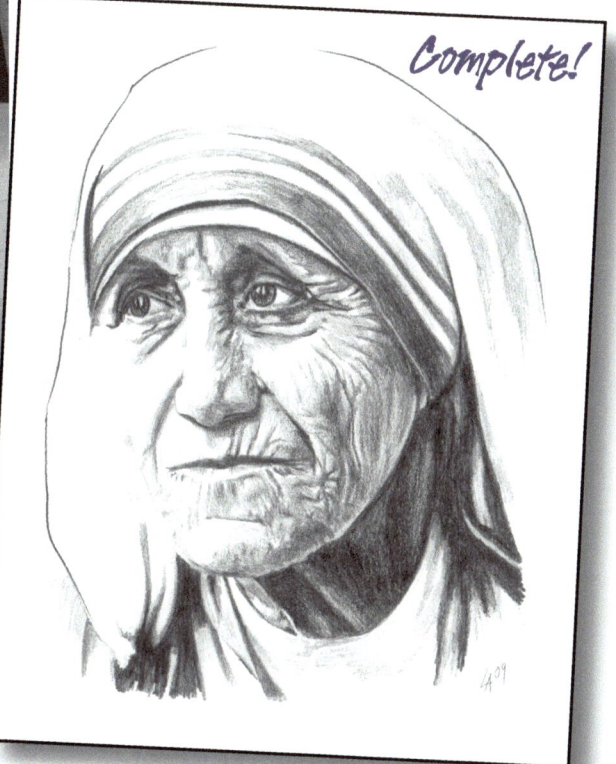

Complete!

To see a demonstration on the Harry Potter Drawing at:
http://www.**youtube**.com/**LindaLaforgeArt**

Anyone Can Draw in Ten Sessions

The Cardinal Rule of Drawing!

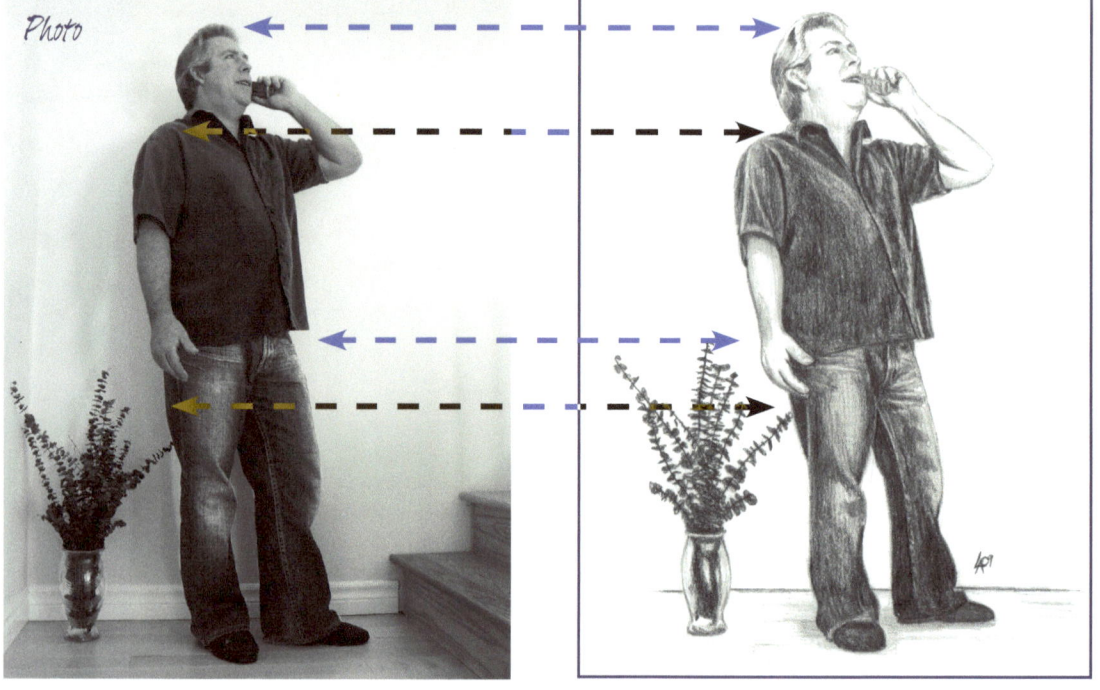

Photo

As you see, I drew my husband on the coffee table, where I gave him his fat head!

Here's a hint at next weeks exercise. I originally drew my husband. My drawing table wasn't available at the time, so I did this on the coffee table in the living room. As I drew, I checked for size, angle and so forth. I thought he looked pretty good too! I added value. I left it. When I looked at it a few hours later I realized I gave him a fat head. You know, I couldn't figure out how I managed to do it when it suddenly hit me. I wasn't looking at my photo or my drawing at the right angle! This goes back to a point made earlier about the angle of your drawing paper and your subject, beit from a photo or still life objects.

Exercise

If you haven't finished your portrait, work to complete it. If you did, do another one.

You may be surprised by this, but faces with more character lines are easier to draw accurately. Less features mean less shapes to seek and compare.

Note: Next Session requires a full body image of someone you'd like to draw next week!

Warm-up Exercise

Warm up drawing exercise! I hope you're excited....

Two 5 minute drawings

1 - Draw as though you're 5 years old and you're giving your picture to Santa

2 - Draw the same object. This time you're an alien to this world and you've only ever seen this thing on a monitor from your home planet before.

> ### This Session we're focusing on:
> • How to Draw People – Proportions, Body Structure
> • Drawing using all your new tools

Capturing a Figure – Body Structure

Do you see any similarities here? Even the Stick Man has evolved!

Exercise 1
(10 minutes)

Draw Stick Men! Draw the stages of his evolution as you see below. Do you see him developing structure? Do you see how you can make his hips swivel like a real person's would? How would his rib cage move? Draw a bunch of stick men in different poses. Don't be afraid to look at how people sit, or stand or walk while drawing your stick men.

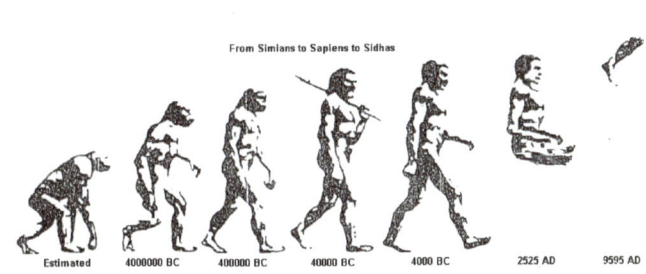

Evolution images found online - artists unknown

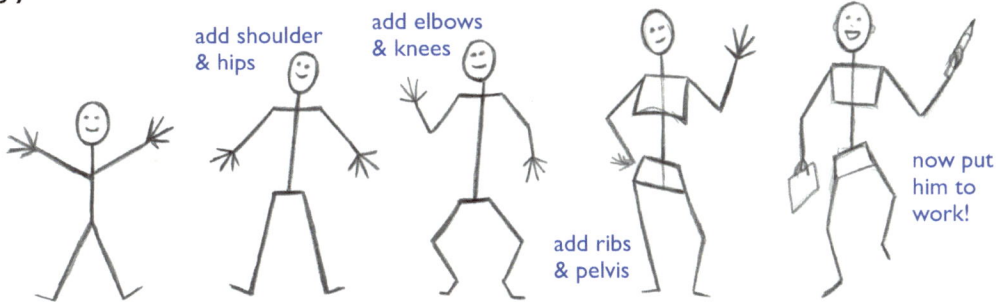

add shoulder & hips

add elbows & knees

add ribs & pelvis

now put him to work!

To see the Evolution of a Stickman at: http://www.**youtube**.com/**LindaLaforgeArt**

Anatomy 101 – or should I say 1701?

The image on your right was drawn by a fellow named Albinus in the 1700's. It's a long way after Leonardo D'Vinci started drawing corpses, however, he is known as one of the most accurate artists in the 'genre'. These guys helped us to see bone structure, organ placement, muscle mass and even blood flow. These are the kinds of things we need to keep in our mind's eye when drawing the human body.

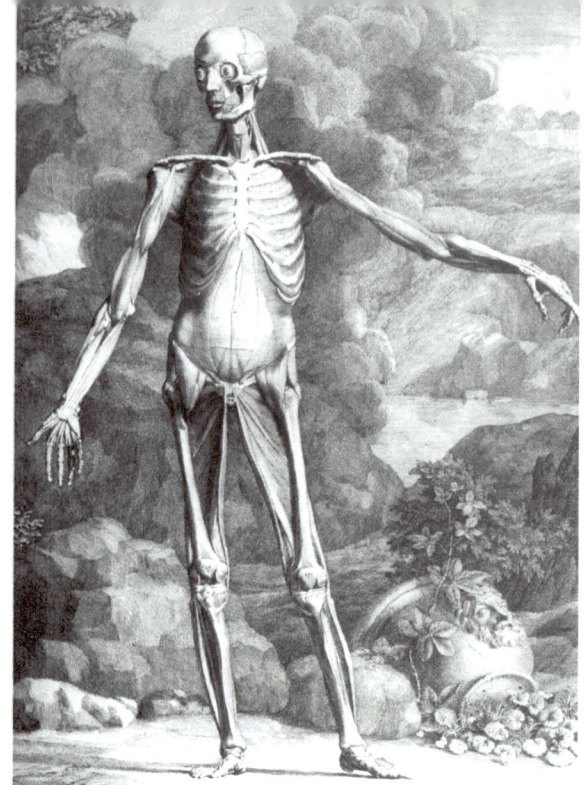

Studying images from medical images and, way easier on the eyes, exercise mags and books help develop a visual 'mind map' that teaches you to shut off your *Intellectual Brain*. Boys, if you have a hankering for the nudey mags, at least now you can tell your woman (or Mom) you're training your brain to draw people better!

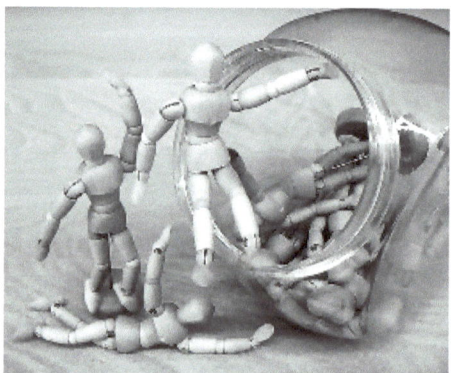
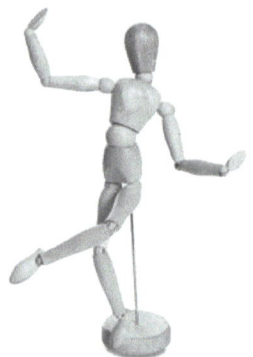

Figurines

Figurines are often used by artists who want to draw a completely original character. I've seen a few types, as shown above. You can use which ever you like when you're ready to stop copying exactly what you see and try creating your own people.

Practice makes perfect. When using models, I suggest you find some who can stay still long enough for you to get them down on paper, or photos. (I like photos!)

People and animals are the most challenging subjects to draw. They are filled with shapes. They've got bone structure – you can see jaw lines, cheek bones, rib cages, knee caps, and so forth. To get them right, get a good understanding of how a person is 'put together'. When you draw a full body, as with anything else, you get the angles and size and proportions on your page. Then you Measure one shape to the next. If you don't take your time in this early stage of your drawing, it won't look right. Get the details right before you start adding values, as you would in any other drawing.

Exercise 2

(2 hours – another worthy challenge!)

Draw a person, from head to toe!
Remember your drawing steps?

The stage of your figure drawing:

1 Angles & shapes

2 Size on your Page

3 Measure as you add in your shapes
 – think of the structure, weight,
 texture, etc...

4 Add Detail to your Shapes

5 Add Value - Shading

Work from a photo!

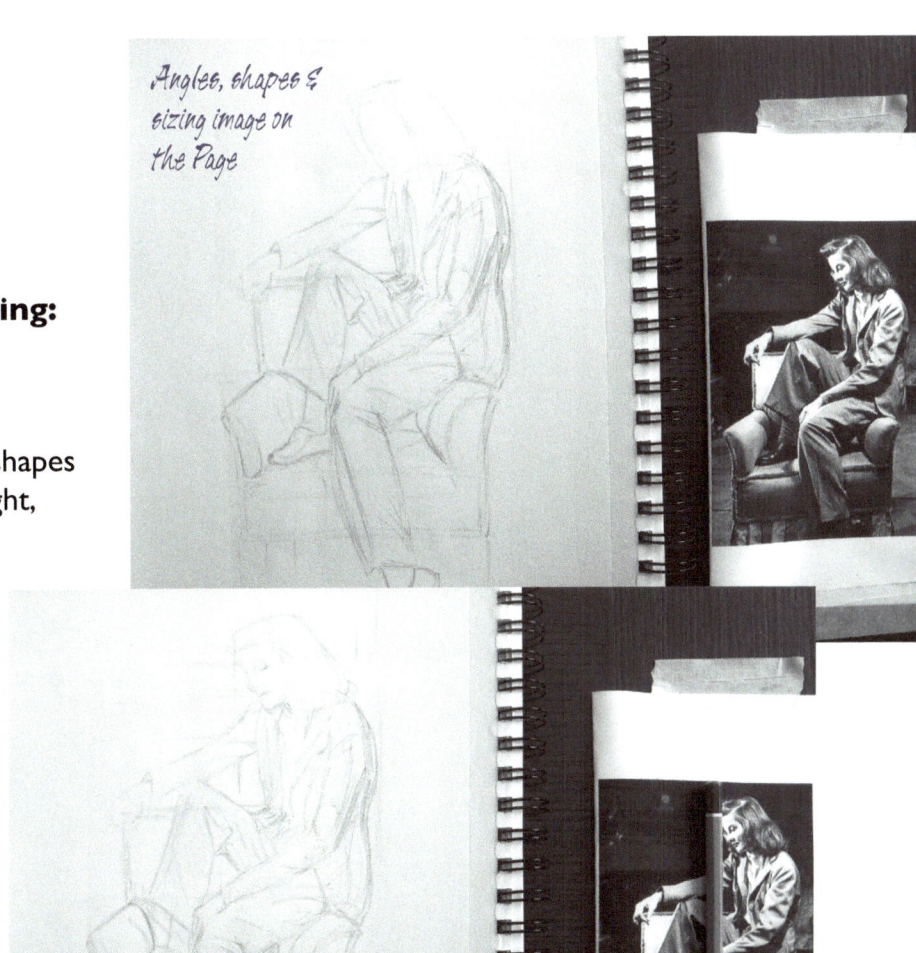

Angles, shapes & sizing image on the Page

Measuring & adding shapes to her face. I'm using the fireplace to help measure her proportions correctly, even though I don't plan on drawing it...

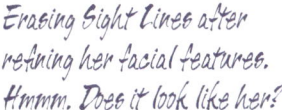

Erasing Sight Lines after refining her facial features. Hmmm. Does it look like her?

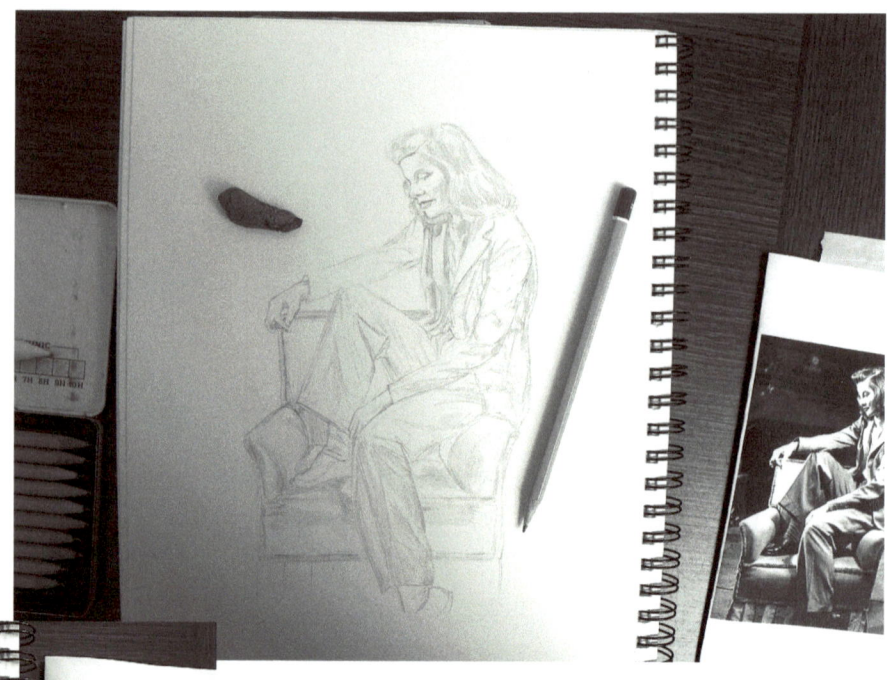

Using my B pencil to add the next darkest shade of value

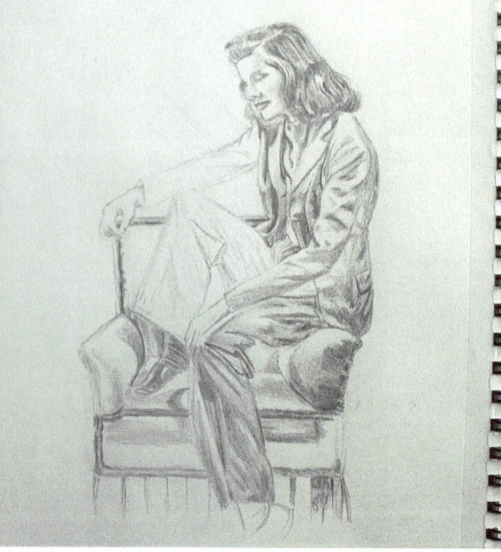

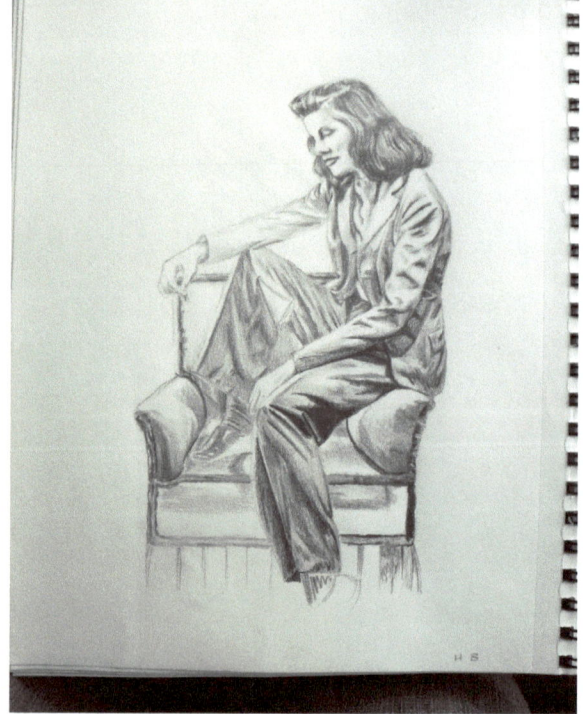

Last step! Using my 5B to add the darkest value, giving it that umph.

If you follow the usual steps you should have no trouble drawing one whole human! You will find yourself erasing your working lines until you have the right proportions.

As most artists, I look at this one and can see room for improvement. My goal here was to make sure this looked and felt like a drawing.

Key! I'm left handed. I work from right to left to avoid smudging. If you're right handed it may help you to work left to right. I also use workable fixative spray!

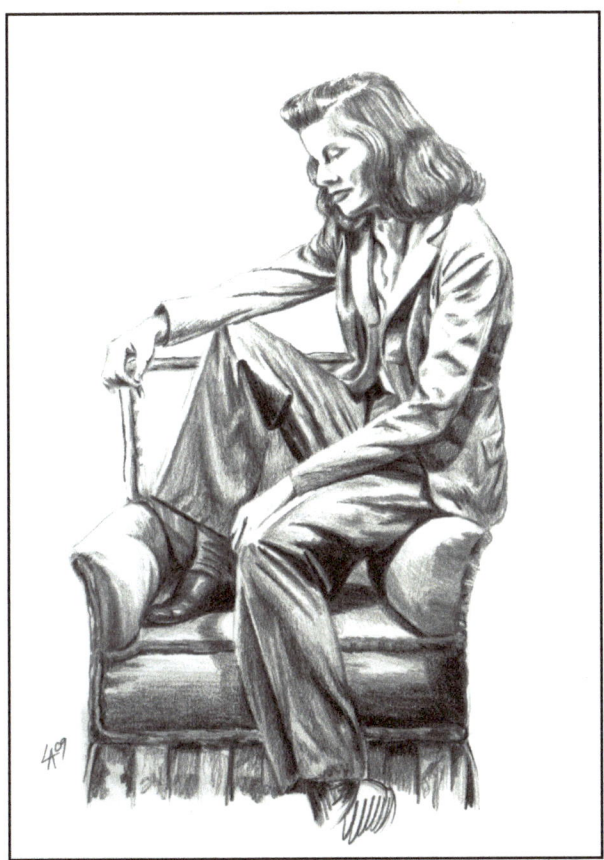

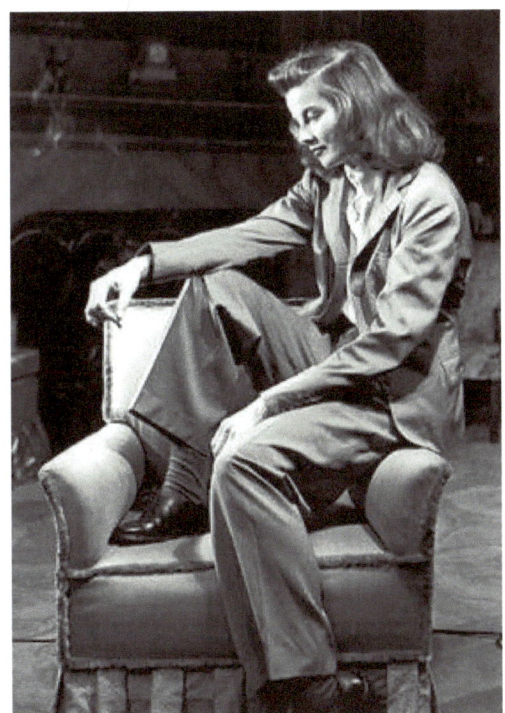

Note: Next Session we're drawing an animal, so find a photo of your favourite beasty!

Session Ten

Warm-up Exercise

Warm up drawing exercise! It's the big day....

Two 5 minute drawings

1 - Draw what ever you want!

2 - However you want

> ### This Session we're focusing on:
> • Drawing Animals OR Anything You Want!
> • Discuss anything you want to about Drawing
> *- People, Animals, Still Life, Shading, Shapes, Sight Lines...*

Drawing Animals - Basic Structure Technique

This is a basic introduction to drawing any kind of animal. It's simple! Use basic shapes to help develop the structure of the animal you want to draw. We learned how to seek the shapes within an object, and how to organize objects within a shape to draw. By using those skills when drawing a cat, or a turtle you can draw a believable creature.

Understanding it's structure can make your little bunny or crocodile jump off the page!

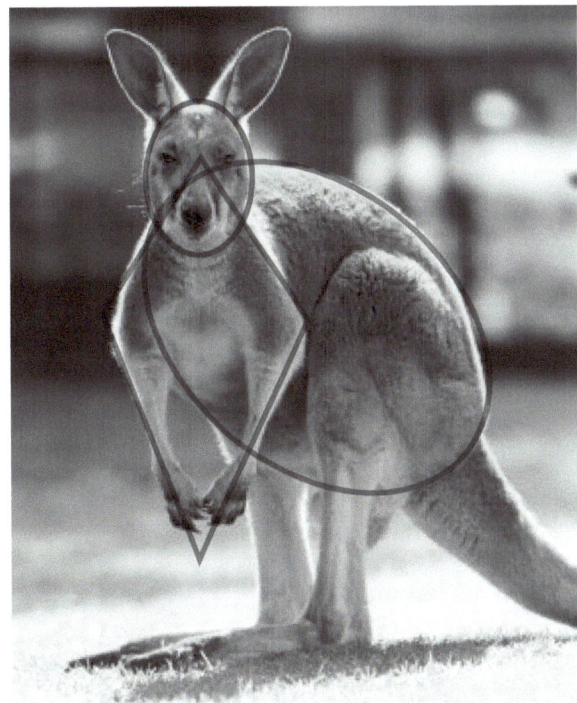

Drawing Animals - same steps as anything else!

Exercise 1

(2 hours – have fun!)

Draw an animal, from head to toe!
Remember your drawing steps?

The stage of your figure drawing:

1 Angles & shapes

2 Size on your Page

3 Measure as you add in
   your shapes – think of the
   structure, weight, texture,
   etc...

4 Add Detail to your Shapes

5 Add Value - Shading

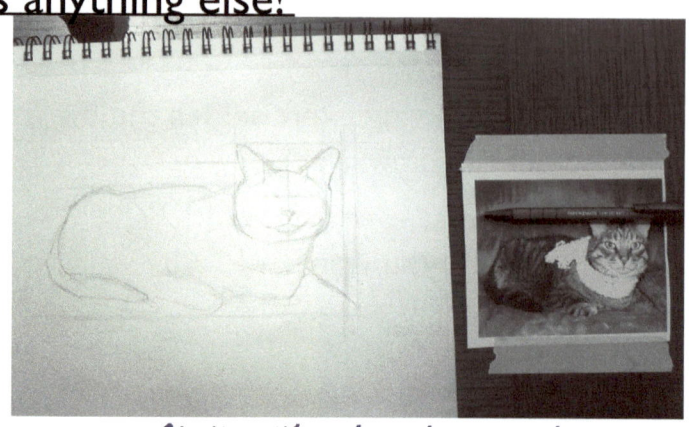

*Starting with angles and sizing my drawing,
measuring and adding the shapes in my cat.*

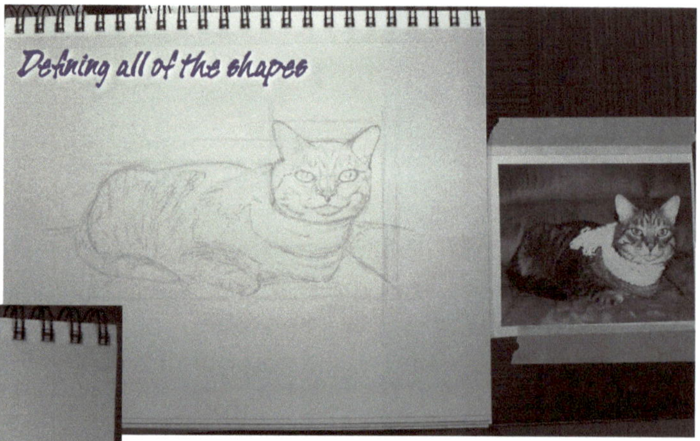

Defining all of the shapes

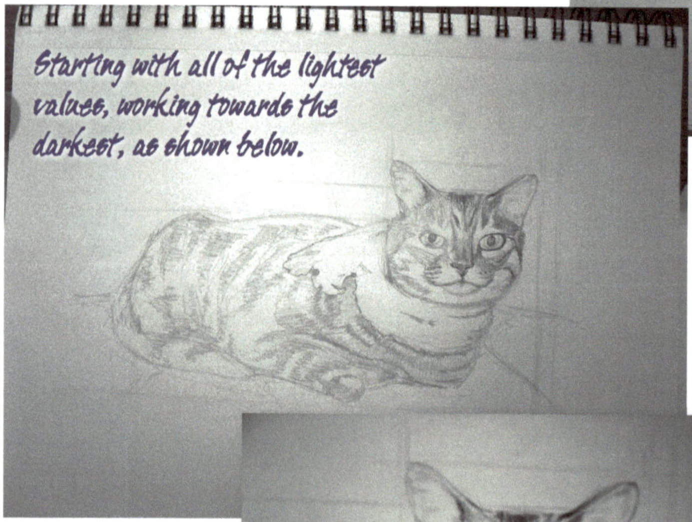

*Starting with all of the lightest
values, working towards the
darkest, as shown below.*

*Adding the
Darker Values*

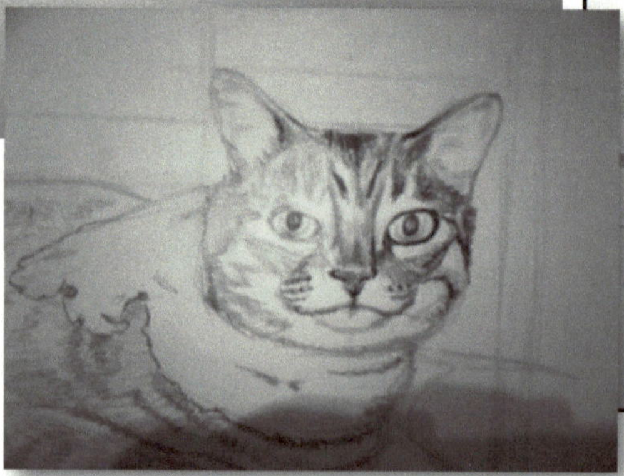

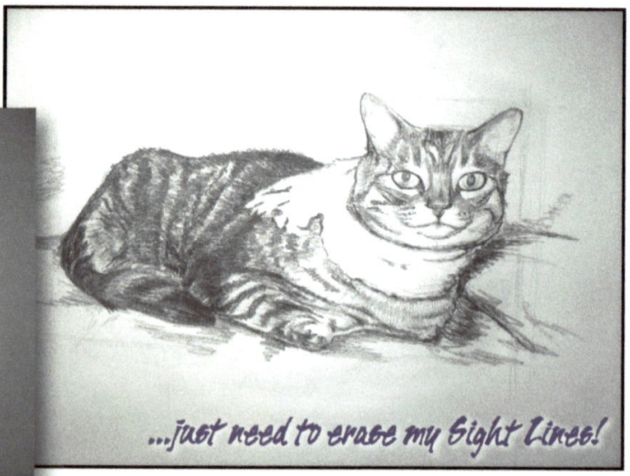

...just need to erase my Sight Lines!

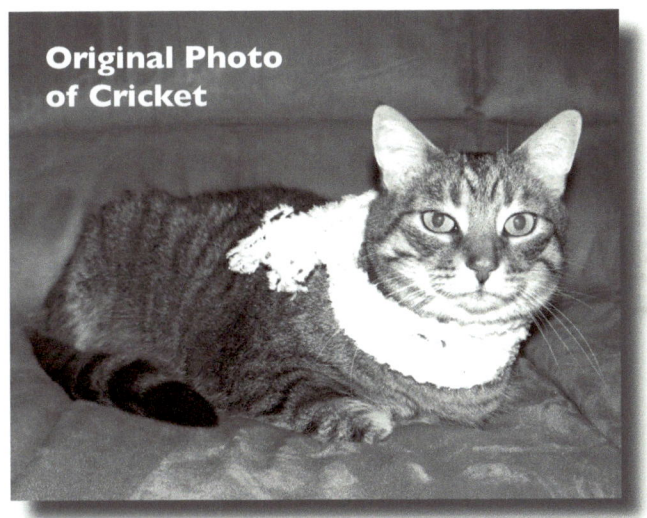

Original Photo of Cricket

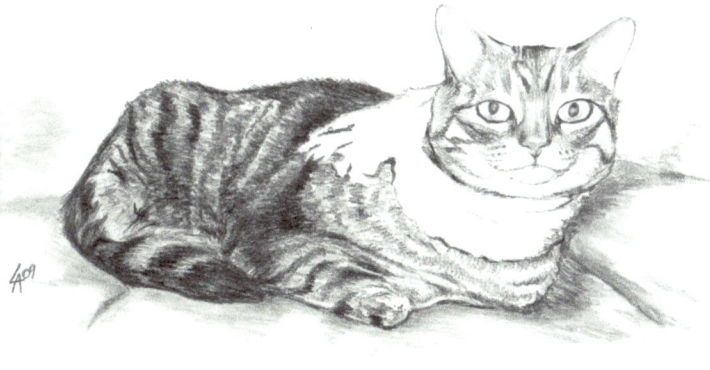

Complete!

Do you notice anything about this drawing? Cricket is a little long. If her head was taller she would look much more accurate. This is a great example of a good, but inaccurate drawing. Consider your drawings 'studies of your subjects'! Even the pros don't get it perfect 100% of the time!

Let's Compare!

Let's compare the drawing you did on Day One with your favourite from one of these Ten Sessions! Look at your major triumphs and give yourself some credit!

You did great!

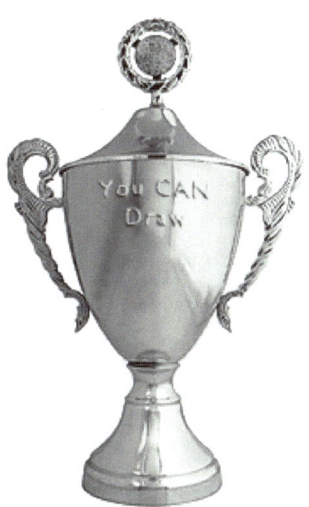

Feedback: Join our Facebook Group and share your drawings for feedback. Posting your drawings within the group will gain you greater insight and even more drawing tips & techniques! You're guaranteed to get constructive and helpful advice from the author and group memebers! You might even be published in the next edition! Visit **www.facebook.com/135512744590** to join today!

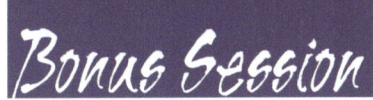

Bonus Session

Yay! You're an Artist!!!!

Now for a few extras, this added chapter offers the new artist a few additional tools and techniques that you can add to your repertoire.

The Extras Section Includes:
• Who Used the Grid Method?
• When one should use the Grid Method
• How to Draw Accurately using the Grid Method

When Artists use the Grid Method

I've been told that artists dating back to the ancient Egyptians knew of a technique to break down a painting into smaller "grids" to effectively divide the image they were creating into a number of smaller images, each of which has less detail than the whole. The "grid method" was even used by Leonardo Da Vinci in both his works and in teaching.

Although I personally believe one can be more expressive in their art without the Grid Method, it's still worth understanding how to do it. I have used it when I've had to reproduce one of my designs on a large outdoor wall mural, and I have taught it. Anyone can use this technique to draw or paint just about anything!

Basic Steps to Grid Drawing

Basically, the grid method is just overlaying a grid onto an original image that you want to draw or paint, and then placing a matching grid pattern on your paper or canvas. As example, if your original image is an 8" x 10" photograph, you could draw a one-inch grid on top the photograph to create a grid pattern with eighty squares (eight squares by ten squares). The original photograph or image is now divided nicely into eighty bite-sized pieces, each being much easier to sketch than the entire original.

You can place a grid on your original in a few ways. One is by placing a grid printed on acetate, a transparent sheet. This keeps one from ruining the original. It's also shiny and takes away from the depth of the image you want to reproduce. I prefer to place a grid on a good copy or print of the original.

Three Steps of Grid Drawing

Step 1. Draw a Grid on a copy of your photo or image. (done for you below)

Step 2. Draw a Grid on your illustration board or drawing paper. Scale it according to the desired size. (done for you below)

Step 3. Copy your photo or image, one square at a time, until you've completed it.

Fun Exercise
(20 minutes)

Use the three steps listed above to drawing the celtic knot below in the grid on the right. Draw one little square at a time.

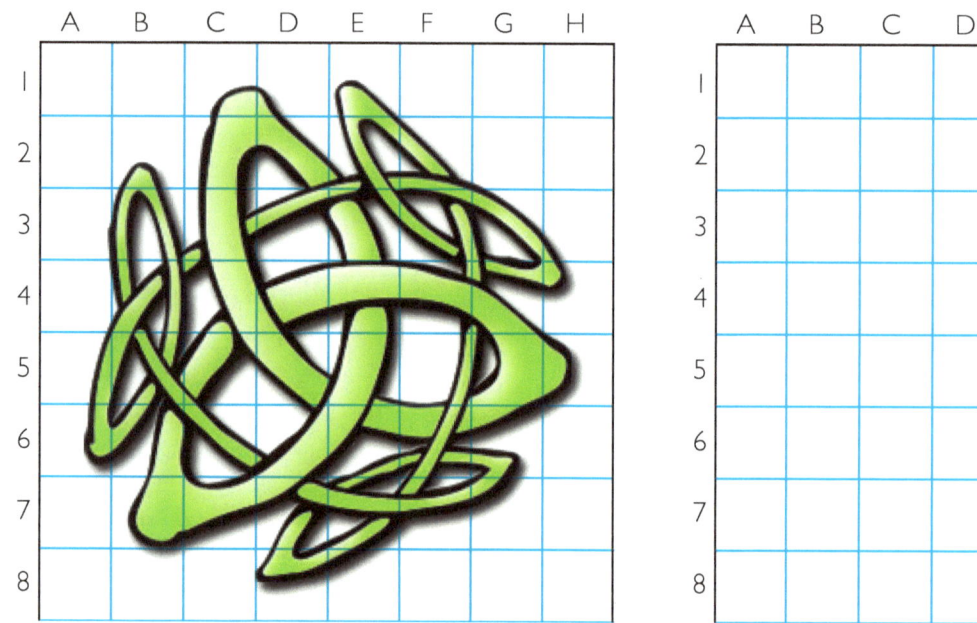

Most artists want to reproduce their original in a larger size. When doing so, the grid is enlarged on the canvas, illustration board or paper. For instance, you may have an 8" x 10" original, but you're painting it on a 16" x 20" canvas. The easiest grid on the original os to draw the squares 1" apart. You can then create a 2" grid on your canvas!

This method is only useful when there is an original image to paint from. An imagined scene or abstract concept is difficult to grid, obviously, since the artist is not working from an original image or photograph. Many beginning artists and art students have learned by painting from an original photo, making the grid method a useful aid in this regard.

Answers to Quick Recap from Page 19

Our history lesson...

True or False

1. Paul Cézanne and Vincent Van Gogh were fabulous artists right from childhood!

   True   **(False)**

2. Cézanne entered the Swiss Academy School of Fine Arts where he learned to draw and paint.

   True   **(False)**

3. Cézanne actually worked very hard, and hung with and learned from the best; Bazille, Renoir, Monet, Sisley and eventually Manet.

   (True)   **False**

4. Cézanne became a great artist, and is popular to this day, because he had passion and he worked at developing his skill and creativity as an artist.

   (True)   **False**

5. Vincent Van Gogh went to a highly reputable school of art in Paris, France.

   True   **(False)**

6. Van Gogh was a risk taker who was willing to explore new methods of painting with colour and passion.

   (True)   **False**

7. While he lived in Paris, Van Gogh met and learned from the best; Fernand CORMON, Emile BERNARD & Henri de TOULOUSE-LAUTREC.

   (True)   **False**

8. Van Gogh created 200 paintings and more than 100 drawings from Feb 1888 to May 1889.

   (True)   **False**

Keep Drawing and keep on exploring your Creativity!
It can be a lot of fun...

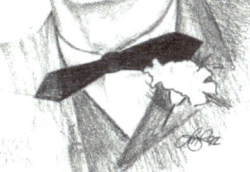

Art Pencils - Leads & Shading (Value)

3H   Light to Dark

2B   Light to Dark

2H   Light to Dark

3B   Light to Dark

1H   Light to Dark

4B   Light to Dark

H   Light to Dark

5B   Light to Dark

F   Light to Dark

6B   Light to Dark

HB   Light to Dark

7B   Light to Dark

B   Light to Dark

8B   Light to Dark

Anyone Can Draw in Ten Sessions